Not a Broken Girl

Mindee Berg

Copyright © 2021, Mindee Berg

All rights reserved. No part of this book may be used or reproduced by any means, graphic, electronic, or mechanical, including photocopying, recording, taping or by any information storage retrieval system without the written permission of the publisher except in the case of brief quotations embodied in critical articles and reviews.

Unless otherwise indicated, all Scripture quotations are taken from the King James Version of the Bible.

All scripture quotations marked NIV are taken from the Holy Bible, New International Version, Copyright © 1973, 1978, 1984 by the International Bible Society. Used by permission.

All scripture quotations marked NIV are taken from the Holy Bible, New International Version, Copyright © 1973, 1978, 1984 by the International Bible Society. Used by permission.

All scripture quotations marked AMP are taken from the Holy Bible, Amplified, Copyright © 1954, 1958, 1962, 1964, 1965, 1987, 2015 by the Zondervan (subsidiary of News Corp) and The Lockman Foundation. Used by permission.

All scripture quotations marked ESV are taken from Holy Bible, English Standard Version, Copyright 2008 by Crossway. Used by permission.

Not a Broken Girl

ISBN-13: 979-8712767830

Edited and formatted by Water2WinePress Publishing House:
a Subsidiary of Ink Well Spoken
www.inkwellspoken.com
Book cover designed by Randy Hill

DEDICATION

To Jill:

Time after time since I was a teenager, you were there beside me when I was struggling. You encouraged me, prayed for me, and pushed me to seek God's truth. Without you, this book would have never come to fruition; because of you, others will find hope and healing. Thank you for being a vessel that God used in my life. Times have not been easy, yet you continue to point others toward Christ. You have left an imprint in my life that will always be there. I am forever thankful for you!

To Kathy:

Though you left this earth too soon, I know you are singing in heaven with the voice of an angel. Your life is the perfect example of what Jesus wanted us to do on this earth. You completed all He had for you here, yet everything you did will have a lasting effect for eternity. You spread His love to all you encountered, and I was blessed to be on the receiving end of it. You were my friend, my bridesmaid, my travel buddy and my sister. Your smile and laugh were infectious, and your hugs were a total comfort! You will always be a part of my heart and story.

TABLE OF CONTENTS

DEDICATION   p.   iii

INTRODUCTION   p.   1

CHAPTER ONE:
THE DAY MY STORY CHANGED   p.   11

CHAPTER TWO:
THAT SMARTS!   p.   23

CHAPTER THREE:
DARK PASSENGERS   p.   29

CHAPTER FOUR:
REJECTING THE NORMS   p.   39

CHAPTER FIVE:
CONFESSIONS & FORGIVENESS   p.   55

CHAPTER SIX:
THE BIG PICTURE
IS HARD WORK   p.   67

CHAPTER SEVEN:
THE "RESET" OF MY STORY   p.   83

CHAPTER EIGHT: **WRONG AGAIN**	p.	95
CHAPTER NINE: **MARRY GO ROUND**	p.	109
CHAPTER TEN: **FROM DARK PASSENGERS** **TO DARK CHOCOLATE**	p.	125
CHAPTER ELEVEN: **UNBROKEN**	p.	135
EPILOGUE	p.	153
ADVICE FOR YOUTH LEADERS	p.	161
BOOK SUGGESTIONS	p.	171
HOTLINE NUMBERS	p.	173
ABOUT THE AUTHOR	p.	175

INTRODUCTION

I was sitting in a Psychology class my freshman year of college at Indiana Wesleyan University (IWU) when what I was hearing began to reveal a destructive path I had been on for the majority of my life. A path that led back to one definitive moment. I wasn't oblivious to this moment that had been coursing through my existence to this point. After all, I was drawn to take this class to get a better grip on healing and hope. What was crazy was that even though I didn't agree 100% with all of their methods, the theories of these world-renowned psychologists began to speak directly to what I had been through; allowing my experiences and choices to make so much more sense even in hindsight.

I began realizing that the sexual abuse I faced as a child started an infection in my heart that just kept spreading over the years into my adulthood. What I thought was a one-time incident actually pushed me to many other abusive situations that crippled the core of who I thought I was as the cycle repeated itself over and over again. I'll share more of my story later, but right now – I need you to know why I chose to write this book.

I was 33 years old when I finally found hope in my traumatic experience. I had just finished getting my second degree in college. I was at a point where I was asking God what He wanted me to do with this degree.

One of my mentors from high school was a woman by the name of Jill. One day, Jill contacted me and said that she had some teens in her youth group come and tell her they had been sexually abused. She wanted to know if there were any books for them to read from a teenage perspective because all she could find were books for adult survivors of sexual abuse. After I did my own unsuccessful research, Jill asked if I could write a letter to the girls: something to give them some encouragement. I wrote the letter, but God kept urging me to write more every time I attempted to end the letter. He made it very clear that I needed to write something for those teenaged girls to help give them hope.

This book is the result. Although the pages that follow are geared towards first-person survivors, they're also for youth leaders, friends and family members of teens who have been abused: the ones who walk alongside their loved ones through the healing who need a better understanding of what that loved one is going through.

It's also very important to convey that everyone's story of abuse is different. I have no doubt that my story is not at all like yours. You may have had a family member abuse you while someone else experienced abuse with a complete stranger. It could have happened once or many times over the course of many years. You may be thinking, "But she doesn't understand my story. My story is worse…" or "My story isn't as bad as all that. My circumstances aren't the same and she and I are two completely different people." Please hear me when I say this: It does not matter! It only takes one time for trauma to manifest. The recurrence of such violations along with how well-trusted the perpetrator was by the victim are important factors – but one time is enough to cause long-lasting damage if unaddressed.

I grew up feeling that my story was so unique that it applied to no one else but me. That was a trick of the enemy to isolate me from both the help I needed and the help I'm able to provide. The thing is, God's truth, grace, mercy and love apply to us all and will never change. As I tell my story, you may only see just a glimpse of yourself or someone you know… and that's enough! I am more than an overcomer in Christ Jesus which means the strength I possess is not my own and is quite transferable! I'm telling you this so that you will see that there is hope! Hope that your future is not defined by your past. Hope that you can be restored and loved so deeply that you will never feel fear again!

A quick disclaimer: I am neither a licensed psychologist nor a theologian. I make no claim to have all of the answers. What and who I am is a child of God who has been given a word to share with you. A word that I believe can help you start your path to healing and hope. I am a person who has a huge amount of compassion for those who have been hurt in any way by sexual abuse. That's just how effective ministry works. What the Lord healed in you was never meant for only you. Your testimony of recovery and restoration is the spirit of prophecy for many others to know (see Revelation 19:10c)!

Before getting into the full content of this book, I want to make sure we're all on the same page in understanding what sexual abuse is. Sexual abuse happens when a person is used for the sexual pleasure of a more powerful person. The goal of the perpetrators is to have pleasure where their victims have no choice but to submit to their desires. Many times, the perpetrator has bound them to some type of secrecy. The perpetrator could be a relative, a stranger, a friend's older sibling or many other possibilities. When victimizers do this, age is not a factor. Rather, they do not have to be significantly older than their victims.

All that matters is that someone has forced some type of power over another person to violate their body. I have seen many different statistics saying how many girls and boys are sexually abused before the age of eighteen. Suppression and secrecy from the shame causes many to admit this long after the abuse took place which makes it hard to really know how accurate the numbers are. What I can tell you is that if you're in a room of 20 people, there will be at least 4 girls and 3 boys who have been sexually abused. More than likely, that number is higher which is devastatingly sad. If only more people knew that we are not alone.

Sexual abuse is also something that doesn't always involve touch. It can be visual or emotional. For example, an adolescent is in the shower and a friend's older brother comes in and watches. As he stands there, the purpose he has is for his own pleasure. That adolescent has now had their honor and dignity violated without having a choice in the matter. That is sexual abuse.

One thing to understand about the human body is that the genitals and breasts have many nerve endings. That's why we become aroused when those areas are touched. This is how God created our bodies. If you look at the beginning of Genesis 50:20 it says:

> "You intended to harm me, but God intended it for good…" (NIV)

This Scripture is Joseph talking about the harm that his brothers caused him, but that God was using it for His good. We can apply that in the way that God made our bodies so that we could have amazing sex lives inside of marriage. Unfortunately, there are many people who will take what God meant for good and use it for bad purposes. When sexual abuse is happening, it is very normal and possible to be aroused even if you are not wanting it to happen. People feel very guilty for that but need to understand that it does not mean that they wanted it or that they were in agreement with it.

I once heard Dan Allender – a prominent Christian therapist, author, professor and speaker who focuses on sexual abuse and trauma – say the following:

> "You cannot change what you will not name."

If you read this book and see even a part of your story, then the only way for your healing to start and for your life to change is for you to name it. It starts as simply as admitting:

"I have been sexually abused."

Maybe you're not there yet and that's okay; but by the end of this book, I pray that you can name your pain, forgive your assaulter and live a fuller life!

To increase its impact, I encourage you to journal as you read this book. For this reason, at the end of each chapter, I will have some questions for you to think through in a section that will be named: Journal Thoughts. Take time to process something you read from the previous chapter. If you notice something that brings a question to your mind or you feel your emotions start to rise – write it out. There are also times when I will reference Biblical scriptures. When you see that scripture, I encourage you to write it down. Write about how that scripture applies to you, and how it makes you feel. Journaling through your feelings can help you understand yourself a little better as it begins to usher in healing.

> God, I pray that You bless the person reading this book right now! Bless their eyes and hearts as they read it; and let Your truth penetrate through the hardness of hurt. Let it penetrate through the fear, shame and guilt that holds so many captive. Even now, put a glimpse of hope in their hearts. Let them feel Your arms of love
>
> wrapped around them. Open their minds to the truth You have for them. Let this be just the beginning of their amazing story of life change,

in Jesus' name! Amen!

Journal Thoughts:

- Is there anything that you are afraid of as you start reading this book? Write down some fears you may have.

- Do you have any hopes for reading this book? Journal through those hopes and pray expectantly for them.

- Is there anyone you trust (a "safe person") that you can talk to as you are reading this book? Write down some names and pray about talking with them and sharing things you learn.

* names have been altered to protect the identity of the involved parties *

JOURNAL YOUR JOURNEY

THE DAY MY STORY CHANGED

"For you created my inmost being; you knit me together in my mother's womb. I praise you because I am fearfully and wonderfully made; your works are wonderful, I know that full well. My frame was not hidden from you when I was made in the secret place, when I was woven together in the depths of the earth. Your eyes saw my unformed body; all the days ordained for me were written in your book before one of them came to be."
– *Psalm 139:13-16 NIV*

Psalm 139 is one of my favorite passages of scripture – and these few verses always grab me. There is not one part of me (or you, for that matter!) that has ever been hidden from God. Think about that. There's a comfort I feel in knowing that He put every aspect of who I am together in the womb of my mother before I was ever born. All the days of my life were written down while my amazing mother was wondering who the child in her belly would become.

My story begins with hers. My parents married young. They lived near Dayton, OH where I was raised and have remained there in that general area to this day. I have no doubt as to the love that they felt for one another. They didn't wait too long to have children because my brother Randy was born a year and a half after their marriage. I came along just a few short years later. Back then, they didn't have a way to tell you the sex of your baby until it was born but I know that deep down, my Mom dreamt of having a little girl. God had already written down my life at this point; and His plan was set in motion. We became a family of five once my little brother Eric joined the party. I was four years old when he was born. Eric rounded out our trio of making forts and playing kickball in the backyard! Many times, it was hard being the only girl. They never wanted to play the girly things like Barbie and Strawberry Shortcake. While I gave into and enjoyed playing boyish things like Star Wars; other times, I was on my own or had to find a neighbor girl to play with me.

I personally think I was born to the best parents anyone could ask for on this green earth. It's not that my parents were perfect people or were righteous in every way. God knew He could use every good and bad choice they made to help me serve the purposes that He had for me. From that perspective alone, I have been blessed beyond measure with my parents! Not many people can say that. Now, I already know what you're thinking… "Mindee, you had it so easy! I can't relate to you!" Or maybe some of you can. The point I want you to see is that it doesn't matter if you had the perfect family or the most jacked up family. Abuse can happen to anyone! Rain falls on the just and unjust alike (see Matthew 5:45).

As far as my relationship with my family, I'm the first

to admit – it wasn't always perfect. There were times when I would have rather moved as far away as I could get; but everyone has had those moments, right? My Mom was raised in a Bible-believing home where she was brought up knowing Who God was and readily accepted the need to have a relationship with Him. My Dad did not come into a relationship with God until he met my Mom. When they got married, they committed their relationship to God and committed to raising children that they entrusted to God. That's something not everyone is blessed to have.

We were raised going to church. My parents were always very involved and had us involved, too. Though the church we grew up in wasn't large, most of our family friends went to the same church as we did. This meant it was one of those congregations where everybody knew everybody. My mom had a beautiful voice which she lent to the choir and other musical specials often. My brother Randy sang in front of the church like my Mom; and since I always had to do what he was doing, I eventually began singing, too. To this day, we both still sing in church and consider it a big part of who we are in ministering to others.

I always knew Who God was and that He was a big part of my life. I honestly don't remember a time of my life where I did not have a belief in God. I accepted that Jesus could help me connect a personal relationship with God the Father at the age of six one summer at Vacation Bible School. It was then that I felt God calling me into this relationship with Him. That was the best thing that has ever happened to me! It was life changing in that I was given eternal life and a Friend that would stay by my side forever. That same summer that I had this awesome experience of meeting Jesus is the same summer that something else happened at that church. It was something that would change my life forever, as well; only with an opposite effect.

When you're six years old, summer is supposed to be full of fun and playing outside with your friends. There was this one specific summer day that I remember very clearly. At the same time, there are some other things about that day that I don't remember. This memory lapse could be that I was six years old and just can't remember everything… or it could be because my mind is trying to protect myself from trauma. Here are some things I do remember. There was a meeting going on at the church during the day; it was either after church during a weekday or on a Saturday. I know this because all the adults were at this meeting while the older kids in youth group were watching the younger kids. It was a really hot day outside and everyone was told we had to stay outside. My best friend was there with me that day. We did everything together!

I've never been a person who likes to be hot and sweaty. Our church didn't have a lot of trees in the area where we were playing so there was nowhere to sit in the shade… and it was hot! I remember I was sitting on the ground in the middle of a large grassy area by myself. I was sweating and bugs were flying around my head. I was so hot and frustrated! I looked up to see my best friend going inside with Micah, one of the older teenage boys who was watching us. Micah said they were going inside because it too hot for them to play games. I remember feeling a little jealous because I wanted to go inside where there was air conditioning, too! I stayed behind at first because I didn't want to be a tagalong. But just as they reached the door, I caught up to them and asked if I could join. Micah said I could but only if I didn't tell anyone else because we were not allowed to be inside. As long as I was okay with that, I was told I could come along with them. This is the day that sexual abuse became a part of my story.

I'm not going to go into details of everything that happened that day, but there are a few things that I will mention because it has a lot to do with the person I became. I couldn't tell you the time span of when this happened. It could have been a few hours but to me it felt like it was all day. In the basement of our church, there was some construction going on. It smelled like saw dust and paint. There were sheets up around certain areas. Some of those areas had tables and some areas had chairs. We were taken to "play our games" behind one of those areas hidden by sheets. Micah would have one of us watch out for people while he took the other to "play." He told us that if we saw someone coming in that we needed to run in and tell him so we wouldn't get in trouble. Other times, if he was feeling especially playful, Micah actually had both of us together with him without a lookout. What was going through my head as these games were being played?

I had the naiveté of a child, as any six-year-old would. I remember thinking parts of the day were fun. It really was like a game. I had no idea that what was happening to me was wrong. Micah repeatedly told us we couldn't tell anyone; but I just thought it was because he would get in trouble for taking us inside where the construction was taking place. There were times when I didn't understand the game but kept playing because I felt like I was supposed to. I remember what I was wearing that day. It was a sun suit – one of those one-piece outfits. The shorts and top were connected with elastic at the waist and it had ties on the shoulders. At one point, Micah had me alone and he wanted me to take off my outfit. He was trying to untie my outfit at my shoulder. I remember that was the one time that day that I felt really scared. I didn't want it to come off. In fact, I told him it couldn't come off because my Mommy had told me not to take it off. I remember feeling almost numb. I couldn't move, and part of me wanted to cry or shout, "Stop!" – but I couldn't. I was frozen. He would do or say something to lighten the mood so that I would feel okay. As a result of Micah violating my space and consent, I had many times where I would freeze up as an adult when someone would touch me as the scared feelings of my six-year-old self rushed back to me.

While Micah had us take turns "playing" with him one-on-one at first; eventually, he got bold enough to be with both of us at the same time since no one came looking for us. At one point, that boldness led to him pushing both of our heads down to his groin area at the same time. I remember my teeth ended up hitting my friends' teeth. In my older mind, I can't comprehend being okay with that; but as a child who was with someone who had power over me that I was supposed to trust, I thought I was okay. I thought I was safe. It's crazy the things you do and don't remember. It's all crazy the things you will focus on to take your mind off the bigger issue. Afterwards, my best friend told me that when Micah was alone with her, he slipped ice from his mouth into hers as he was kissing her. Instead of thinking, "Eww, how gross," I thought, "Why didn't he kiss me? What's wrong with me?" I was even a little jealous. That thought has haunted me my entire life in three ways:

1. Why on earth would I have even wanted that?
2. I began to base my worth on how someone else felt about me.
3. I began identifying whether or not someone liked me based on whether they physically expressed it.

Let me explain. I rationalized that something must be wrong with me if another person didn't like me or a guy I liked didn't kiss me. As I got older, I found myself doing whatever I could to get a guy to kiss me. So, not only was it what Micah did to me; it was also what he didn't do to me that affected how I felt about myself when interacting with the opposite sex.

When it came down to it, we both walked away feeling like we had a secret to protect: a fun day with one of the older boys. And everything would be fine as long as the adults didn't find out about it and no one got in trouble. Neither of us realized just how much we'd been hurt, though. Imagine that – he was supposed to be protecting us but we ended up feeling the need to protect him and his dirty little secret.

I don't remember either of us talking about it anymore until a few years later when we were both riding home on the school bus. It came up as we were talking to a boy our age by the name of Chad. He was transferring to another bus that Micah just so happened to be riding. For some reason, we decided to tell Chad what happened at the church that day. I think we told him because we wanted to show how cool we were by telling him something we'd done that we weren't supposed to doing. We were really telling him like it was something cool that had happened. Chad didn't even believe us.

We told Chad to ask Micah about what we told him. We just knew Micah would back up our story. The next day, we couldn't wait to hear Chad confess that we'd been telling the truth when he got on the bus. But to our surprise, Micah told Chad that we made it all up. I remember feeling so confused. I couldn't understand why Micah would say that. Why would he say it didn't happen? Why would he make us look like liars? We didn't pursue it any further, but it stuck with me. I would play it over and over in my mind trying to figure out if I had made it up. I questioned myself: "Why would Micah say it didn't happen? It's not like we told another adult and got him in trouble. We kept up our end of the bargain… So, why did he lie?"

Journal Thoughts:

- What was your childhood like? Write down a few of your favorite memories.

- Do you have any memories you've tried to forget? Write down a memory that is a struggle for you to think about. Write about how it makes you feel.

- Are you currently being sexually abused by someone? If so, it is important that it stops now! If you identified that safe person I asked you to pray about at the end of the Introduction, then tell them. If you don't have such a person in your life, then please consider talking to a counselor at school or a trusted youth leader.

JOURNAL YOUR JOURNEY

THAT SMARTS!

I grew up in a middle-class family where mom stayed home and raised the children while dad worked. My parents were not rich. My Dad worked hard in sheet metal and construction. It was difficult at times providing enough for the five of us. On top of that, it was important for my parents to send us to a private Christian school. I know that's where most of their money went. Even though we didn't have all the name brand clothes or the nicest cars, I never felt like I missed out on anything. I was blessed to be able to go to Dayton Christian School. No matter where my friends attended from elementary to high school, I had no desire to go anywhere else. I learned a lot at that school about God and my relationship with Him. I also learned a lot of Bible verses! We had scriptures to memorize every week! It's okay though because those scriptures have come to mind so many times over the years. Psalm 119:11 says:

> "I have hidden your word in my heart that I might not sin against you." (NIV)

I can't tell you how having God's Word in my heart has helped when I was struggling! So, at the end of the day, being forced to memorize scriptures while my friends were mesmerized by whatever cool show was on television has been nothing but a blessing for me!

Fourth grade was a pretty defining year for me. I remember that was the year the Challenger exploded. I remember seeing it repeatedly on the television. It was the first national tragedy I can recall. I also remember dentists coming to school to teach us about brushing and flossing our teeth. They gave us a red pill to chew up to show where we missed brushing and still had plaque on our teeth.

One thing that made fourth grade stand out from other years was the Science Research Associates (SRA) Reading Program. This program helped with reading comprehension. You were put at a certain level of reading depending on your score. I was put at the lowest level. Why is that such a significant memory? It stood out to me because it made me feel "less than" my friends. I felt stupid. I felt like I wasn't smart enough to reach the same level as everyone else... and never would be. So, I stopped trying to be smart. I was already a C average student – so this was just one more thing that made me feel like I wasn't enough. Throughout high school and even upon receiving my Associate's degree, I've always maintained a C average – reinforcing this thought that I just couldn't be smart.

Fifth grade was a big year! I was in middle school and this was the year we switched buildings. It was a new building with new friends. I even had a crush on a boy! He was so cute! His name was Jason and he had a crush on me, too. That year on Valentine's Day, while everyone else was getting small cards, Jason gave me a big card! I wasn't sure what to make of that but I liked it! As soon as I knew he liked me, I got really scared.

It's not that I didn't want him to like me. I couldn't figure it out at the time but as soon as he told me he liked me, I was almost afraid of him. This confused me terribly but became the norm for me when it came to boys over the years to come.

One day that year, the school took my class and another fifth-grade class to the guidance counselor to have a serious talk with us. We were guided into this room that had the padded seats where the bottom of the seat swiveled up and down. Needless to say, it quickly became the fun room! I was sitting in the back row with a girlfriend of mine when the counselor started telling us about good touches and bad touches. I honestly don't even remember what the counselor said. I just remember my heart started to sink as thoughts took me back to that ill-fated day at the church. Until then, I hadn't thought about it in years. The memories of that day were hidden away. Locked up in a file cabinet in the deep recesses of my mind. As I pulled out that file and looked through it, I realized that each memory fit the description that the counselor was talking about. I wanted to go tell someone, but there was something bigger than life that stood in my way: a blanket of guilt and shame that covered me from head to toe in that moment.

Shame is a negative emotion caused by the awareness of something wrong you have done. In me, it created an emotional pain that I didn't know how to deal with – I mean, who could at that age? You only need to be abused once to cause shame. I once worked with a girl whose coach would put his hand on her leg when no one was watching. She felt shame from that, and it stayed with her for many years after.

I was eleven at this point, so the guilt and shame came more from the fact that I thought what had happened to me was okay for five years. I even thought it was fun. How could I think that? How could I enjoy something that this world considered so bad? I allowed it to happen, I brought it on myself and no one could ever really love me if they knew I let this happen to me. Those were the thoughts that Satan was whispering in my ear despite all the scriptures I knew. Coupled with embarrassment, the guilt and shame crippled me. I had to do the only thing I could at the time. I had to forget and push it all away.

Journal Thoughts:

- Do you have a time where you've felt shame? Write down 2 or 3 times you felt shame and why.

- Have you ever talked to anyone about those times? Pray God brings to mind someone you can talk to; if you already know a person then set a time to talk with them.

- Have you ever memorized a scripture? Try memorizing Psalm 139:13-16.

JOURNAL YOUR JOURNEY

DARK PASSENGERS

Life in middle school through my college years was filled with a lot of fear, confusion and insecurity. By this point in my life, my subconscious had already trained itself to think, act and react like a broken girl.

To help you understand the state I was in during the formative years of my life, I'd like you to take a second and think about a tree. When you think of this tree, you likely envision its bark. It may be thick, brown and rippled or it may be smooth and white. It may have large green leaves, small red leaves or even beautiful flowers covering its branches. The one part you don't typically see is the roots. They grow complex systems beneath the ground that either run really deep or stay shallow. I've read that the roots of a tree can even be as big as the tree itself. Some root systems are massive enough to come up above ground – cracking up driveways and sidewalks or potentially pushing through the foundation of a house. In essence, what was meant to provide stability can also become a destructive force of nature.

The fruit of a tree is something we typically think of as sweet and nutritional, but it can be harmful, as well. For example, the Manchineel tree bears sweet fruit but it is also incredibly poisonous. Fruit can be deceiving. Fruit also comes and goes in seasons. Sometimes it grows; other times, it just dies off. Though fruit doesn't have as much destructive potential as roots, in many respects, it is an extension of the roots. You see, the fruit couldn't be there without the roots. Both are essential elements of what we know a tree to be.

If I may, I'd like to build something into our tree model. I've come to understand that both the roots and fruit stemming from the sexual abuse I experienced have produced what I like to call "dark passengers." I can't take credit for coming up with this concept, but I have identified them in my life so that you might be able to do the same in your own circumstances. I once saw this show where a guy struggled with an issue that at times, made him feel as broken as I've felt over the years. The issue for him was a sin issue he had chosen to live with. He called his sin issue his dark passenger. Since watching this show, I can't help but think of the roots and fruit of my abuse as my dark passengers.

In taking the time to explain them up front, my hope is that you will have a better understanding of what I mean when they're mentioned later. As roots, dark passengers can be so deep that the only way to get rid of them is through some serious deliverance sessions. To completely address this aspect of healing, I would strongly encourage you to seek out the help of a church with an active deliverance ministry. Like fruit, dark passengers come and go seasonally. They appear good on the outside and even taste sweet initially; but on the inside, the poison they release wreaks havoc on the soul.   There are many different roots and fruits that appear throughout my story. They are unwelcome and nothing but hurtful. I don't want to live with them; but at times, I honestly don't know how to live without them.

When that blanket of shame came over me at eleven, I subconsciously figured out how to manage it. I filtered it through control. As long as I didn't let anyone too close – they wouldn't be able to see that shame. It kind of happened on its own with Jason in the fifth grade. After Jason, I learned how to use it as a defense mechanism against anyone (particularly males) who had the potential of getting close to me. I controlled my own actions to keep people at bay. It can be hard to recognize at first, but eventually that control will manifest itself in different ways with different people. As a quick example, controlling how close someone gets may come out as an eating disorder. Unfortunately, and saddest of all, that control often ends up with the abused becoming the abuser through mental, physical or drug abuse; self-abuse, or even abusing other people in the same way they were abused.

Having established that, let's get back to unpacking my story. My family eventually ended up leaving the church I was abused in for unrelated reasons. We all continued to be really involved in our new church. I sang and helped lead worship. I became a youth group leader and I still really cared about my relationship with God. I just didn't like myself very much nor could I accept how could God love me even though I knew His love was real. I had basically disassociated myself from the truth of His love; choosing instead to believe that it was real for everyone else except me.

In sixth grade, I met my next boy crush by the name of Paul. He was tall, blonde and somewhat of a bad boy type which combined together to make him super attractive! And get this... he was older! Paul was an eighth grader but we had a lot of mutual friends. He was also one of those types who knew the right things to say to make me think I was the most important person in the world. One time, he sent me a note to let me know that he thought I was cute and wished I was in eighth grade with him. Needless to say, that was all it took for me to be totally infatuated with him! If there was a guy that thought I was cute then that must mean I was worth something, right? Aside from having Paul's interest, I had other boys in middle school that asked me to "go with them," too. But what did that really mean? Each time I accepted such attention, a dark passenger would show up to sabotage the connection as fear would roll over my body all over again. It was too real for me. What if they found out who I really was? What if they find out what I had done? What did they expect from me? Did they expect me to do those things that I did with Micah? This was my cycle throughout middle school. Each time the fear reared its ugly head felt like the first. I was too scared.

I began the ninth grade with a lot of excitement. My mom was pregnant with my youngest brother Brett. I was a cheerleader... and I ended up with my first real boyfriend! It ended up being tall and blonde Paul. Though he switched to a public school, we would see each other at school events. This was a time before cell phones and email, so we actually wrote letters and sent them through the mail a few times over the years leading up to me entering high school. He always made comments about how amazing I was and confessed that he wished so badly that I had been allowed to date when I was in eighth grade. Since 99% of our communication wasn't in person, I had a chance to experience someone who wanted me without physical touch. I just knew this had to be the man I was going to marry because he kept telling me everything I want to hear!

Once I was in high school, Paul asked if we could start dating. I was excited but I also knew this meant he had to meet my Dad. I dreaded that day a little because I knew Paul didn't have the best reputation. The day Paul met my Dad was a memorable one. It started off innocent enough. Dad was kind. He shook his hand and made polite conversation… but then he finished it with the one thing every girl prays they'll never hear. He looked Paul right in the eyes and said: "If you hurt my daughter, just know I have a shotgun in the basement… and I am not afraid to use it!" I thought I would die of embarrassment! Paul gave a little laugh. I think he was trying to figure out if Dad was joking or serious. And that's exactly where my dad wanted him!

Our first date night came around and all I wanted to do was throw up. I was so nervous. I wanted to be loved so bad! I wanted to feel like I was worth something… anything. Paul picked me up and had made a mixtape for me that we listened to the entire time he drove to his high school's football game. On the way, he asked if I wanted anything from Arby's (I know big spender, right?!!). I was so nervous – and I knew if I ate, I would throw up! I said I wasn't hungry so he just ordered for himself. By the time we got to the game, I started to get that fearful feeling again. Why? Why, when I wanted this so badly, was I scared to death? I didn't really talk much. I just sat there while he talked to his friends. After the game, he drove me to my high school parking lot where the only thing I remember is him kissing me… and it tasting like Arby's. I've got nothing against Arby's, but it was awhile before I could eat Arby's food again!

We went on multiple dates over the next few months. One night after hanging out, we went to a golf course. We snuck in and sat in a gazebo on the edge of the course. No words were being said. I was too nervous to say the wrong thing. He had his arm around me when he slid his hand up my shirt. This was the first time anyone had touched me in that way since I was six… and I froze. It was obvious enough for Paul to notice because he commented about it:

> "I don't understand why you're so different now. I feel like I can't touch you or even talk to you."

If you recall, our communication had been mostly long distance without being directly in front of each other. I didn't have to worry about any physical touch which allowed me to be much more open and expressive. I had only read that I was worth something to Paul which was a safe place for me. It all changed the moment he translated his feelings into something physical... and now, in that moment, all I felt was that I was being violated again. He didn't understand and honestly, I didn't fully understand it, either. I was just frozen and so afraid of what he would have me do next. What I know now is that once he realized I didn't like his advances, he should've stopped... but he didn't.

Things never went much further with Paul. We went to Homecoming at my high school together. I didn't even want to go but I didn't want my friends to think that Paul didn't like me. If he didn't like me, that would mean I was worthless again. Besides, I had already bought my teal dress with the puff sleeves and my shoes dyed to match! On top of that, my hair was tall and hair sprayed for pictures when he picked me up. No judgement – after all, this was 1990 and that was the style! Meanwhile, Paul had on a sweater cardigan and dress pants on with some janky brown shoes. Later on, my parents made it known that he hadn't even bothered to dress nice or care enough about my outfit to try to match it. After pictures, we drove to the banquet. Don't forget – I went to a Christian school so there was no dancing! We had a banquet with entertainment. That's it. When we got there, we did the professional pictures and walked to our table. As soon as we sat down, my close friend Michelle pulled me aside. She had something important to tell me. The night before, Paul and I were out with Michelle and some other mutual friends at a pizza place. When I got up to use the bathroom, Michelle said that her brother Craig asked Paul how things were going between the two of us. Paul's response was: "Great! I can't wait to spread her!"

I was completely confused at first. There was part of me that didn't think he could say such a thing; but the other part of me almost expected it. Although I should've been angry, I just became sad and fearful as my heart sank. See, I had made a commitment to stay pure until marriage – something I thought he understood and respected. Although he could've just been trying to show off around other boys – in my heart, I was too afraid to risk it. A few days later, I confronted him about what I'd heard but he denied it. He said he would never say that about me, but it was too late. I wanted to be nowhere near him. We broke up a few days later.

Journal Thoughts:

- At this point in my story, my dark passengers were:
    - Fear
    - Self-doubt
    - Self-hatred

  Do you have any dark passengers? Write about them. Name them and talk about how they make you feel.

- Do your dark passengers speak to who you truly are? Find scriptures that tell you the truth and write them. Put them up around your house in places you can see and try to memorize them.

JOURNAL YOUR JOURNEY

REJECTING THE NORMS

The relationship with Paul was the beginning of a long line of abusive relationships that followed in the wake of Micah's sexual assault. While there were guys who took advantage of me emotionally and physically; there were also times when I used men to make me feel better about myself. The abuse now went both ways as I began wielding control as a defense mechanism. By this time, I was so insecure that I would tell guys that they thought I was fat and ugly. I wanted to tell them before they had the chance to tell me. I figured it would hurt less if I put it out there first. I did this with my friends, too. I also did this hoping they would come back and tell me how beautiful I was. As you might imagine, this became an emotionally draining and toxic thing to put on another person.

As I was getting older, there were many times I was burdened by really uncomfortable feelings. The main dark passengers that accompanied me during this season were fear and insecurity. These two often left the door open for confusion and dread to creep in, as well. Case in point: My brother Randy typically drove me home from school but one day, I decided to wave off my brother so I could stay after school and talk to my friends. Walking home wasn't a big deal to me because we only lived a few blocks away from school. However, the neighborhood between my house and the school really wasn't the greatest which is why my Dad arranged for my brother to drive me home. As I was walking home, a car pulled up next to me. A man rolled down the window and tried to talk me into getting in his car. Fear manifested as my dark passenger and, in a moment's notice, invited confusion to come along for the ride. I stood there frozen – unable to talk or move. When Randy got home from school and my dad saw that I wasn't with him, he got really upset. He jumped in our conversion van and sped off to find me. He pulled around the corner and saw me staring into this creepy guy's car. All I remember hearing is the van pull up behind me as I looked up to see my hero jumping out to save the day. When the guy saw my Dad pull up, he put the pedal to the metal and got out of there as fast as he could. All that was running through my mind was that I was about to be abducted and killed. With my Dad there, those dark passengers were subdued by the relief I felt knowing that I was safe in my Dad's presence.

When I finally got my own license, I thoroughly loved the freedom! My first car was an '81 black Ford Escort. It was a stick shift, so my Dad taught me to drive it in the parking lot of my high school. Like any newly licensed teenager, I would look for any reason I could find to drive. But I quickly discovered that driving places wasn't always fun. One time, I went to get gas and there was an older guy at the pump next to mine who looked like he worked some type of construction job. He was dirty and rude. He started whistling at me as he began looking me over. Another time, I was getting gas when some random older guy kept telling me how pretty I was. Though I tried ignoring both of them, fear immediately jumped into my car and went into overdrive. As a result, I absolutely hated going to a gas station by myself for years. I learned the limits of how far I could drive each of my cars with the tank on E; doing everything I could think of to avoid filling up. The very thought of getting out of the car at a gas station with that dark rear passenger was enough to paralyze me. That's why I would always try to have people in the car with me. I would drive my friends to school and school events. I even ended up driving the kids in our neighborhood to our church youth group… and I drove to church a lot! I was the type of teen who was at church as long as the doors were open. More for the social side than the spiritual side, at times. I felt safe there which helped me feel accepted and cared about. Ironically, youth group was the one place that always felt safe for me.

Two of the greatest things about being part of a youth group were the friendships and mentors that you developed over time. Again, I am thankful for these blessings because I realize that many people in my situation don't have them. They are things that I do not take for granted. I met two women during this time in life who, to this day, I still look up to. Jill and Sharlene have been two women who accepted, loved and prayed for me. They gave me great direction and advice – but unfortunately, I didn't always take it in the time I should have. One of the main areas of my life where I was given advice that I didn't use right away was in the boy department. Admittedly, I was known for being boy crazy. We took many ministry trips in youth group; and every trip we went on was an opportunity to look for a boy! I was still trying to find that love and acceptance to make me feel like I was worth something. You see, the boys I met on the road couldn't come home with us or hang around long enough to want a relationship. It would seem that I felt happiest and safest in long-distance, short-lived relationships. The boys and the ministry trips weren't my focus, though. I loved the youth group because I felt most accepted there.

If you recall, I became a cheerleader in high school. In the 80s and 90s, cheerleaders were the "popular" girls. I tried really hard to be accepted with this group, but most of the time, I found myself being laughed at on the outskirts. But I kept trying. I wore all the makeup I could and made my hair as big as I could get it. One year at cheerleading camp, I met a girl from another school. We hit it off really quickly! So much so, that she said she'd drop by my room later to say "Hello." That day had been a particularly sweaty one from all of the routines we practiced, so I decided to shower before she stopped by. I was sitting with some other girls waiting for my hair to dry and there was a knock at the door. I was so excited that my new friend had actually gone out of her way to look for and find me! One of my roommates opened the door as I heard: "Is Mindee here?"

When I got to the door, she just stood there – glaring at me in disbelief. "Oh, I must have the wrong Mindee," she said. All I could think is she didn't (want to) recognize me because of how ugly I looked with wet hair and no makeup. I couldn't even respond to her as she walked away giggling with her friends. Enter the dark passenger of rejection. Even as I reflect on this, I find it interesting that I overlooked the acceptance of the youth group and even my father: rejecting them both for the unattainable acceptance of strangers.

Another instance where I was rejected by the popular crowd arose when I started dating this basketball player. He was part of the popular crowd by default so when he told me that one of his friends asked him why he was dating me because I was ugly – I was devastated. I mean, really?!?!? What guy would say that to his girlfriend? What I took away from that is that there must be only one thing he wanted to use me for since I was so ugly. The one thing that I protected above all costs. Over time, I got to a place where I never travelled alone. Whether walking or driving, my dark passengers became all I could see and feel about myself.

Rejection is an ugly thing. Once you let it in, it invades every part of you. It's not just a feeling. It's an entity that lives inside of you as an enemy waiting to attack and defeat you at every corner. It will take everything someone says and pervert it into a personal and negative assault. Reinjuring and adding salt to the wound that gave it entry in the first place. It's so perverse and tactical, it can even take compliments and twist them into insults. If someone near you is whispering, it'll convince you to automatically think they're talking about you. Rejection breeds paranoia, too. You'll find yourself almost convinced that they must know your secret shame which you'll rationalize as the reason no one (particularly those whose approval you run after) accepts you.

Rejection causes you to make a lot of assumptions, too. Rejection thrives in your mind where your subconscious is. Think of it this way. It's the subconscious mind that sustains your breathing without you having to think about it. It also helps you put one foot in front of the other and balance yourself when walking. The subconscious drives your reflexes and is the operator behind the scenes that makes sure you pull your hand away fast when you touch something hot. Your subconscious starts working before your conscious does and hosts feelings you don't even realize you have. So it makes sense that rejection makes its home in the subconscious. It's like a virus that hijacks a computer's operating system. Viruses corrupt systems and are designed to be malicious. Rejection was my virus and I became very sick from it. Sick enough to feel unworthy of love.

Throughout high school, the same story played out over and over again. Though I mentioned a computer virus before, this cycle reminds me of the type of viruses that attack our bodies. The one thing they're programmed to do is make copies of themselves while spreading an ideal environment for them throughout the body; causing chaos in the process. This was my life. Every situation I encountered with different people ended with the same manifestations. I would be interested in a guy until the moment they liked me back. Once I knew how they felt, I would preemptively reject them before they could reject me. My mode of rejection was the flight response. I would simply run away in fear. My other strategy would be to keep chasing after a guy I liked in hopes that he would make me feel loved and worth something. But as fast as I ran away in my flight response, I would over-pursue him which would, in turn, freak him out and put him on the run. Either way, I would always end up hurt and rejected.

Most of the time, I would be interested in multiple guys at the same time. I guess I was playing the numbers game to increase my chances of finding what I was looking for in a relationship. There was one guy named Mike that I had a big crush on. He was also a really good friend of mine. He didn't have an interest in me other than friendship for a long time. Then I started really liking a guy named Ted. He was also a great friend. One day, I came to my car to find someone had placed a card on my windshield. Though I had hoped it was from Ted, it was Mike who actually sent it. In the card, he professed his love for me. Though that sounds like what I was looking for; I was still disappointed. And just like that, I was done crushing on Mike. One of my friends even confronted me about why I switched off so suddenly once I found out how he felt about me. I couldn't even give her an answer because I didn't know myself. All I knew was that I wanted to be loved by whomever I was focusing my thoughts on at the time. Yet, the second I knew that they actually liked me, I would just switch to liking someone else – prompted internally by rejection.

There were times I would be out and about when a kind looking guy around my age would smile at me. I would instantly think to myself... "He thinks I'm worth something. Maybe he's who I am meant to be with." Meanwhile, if an older looking guy smiled at me, I would instinctively freak out and run away thinking... "He's going to hurt me." The crazy thing that went along with these reactions to strangers was that I began being uncomfortable around the one person who I knew would protect me more than anyone else in this world: my Dad.

How many times have I already mentioned my Dad protecting me? Did I mention the time my parents had me taking lessons at the local swim club? Though I was a basic swimmer at best, I became part of their swim team because they didn't have enough swimmers to compete locally. If you can't already see the set up, this was a recipe for disaster! At the first swim meet, my brain froze as soon as I dove into the cold water. I couldn't tell which way was up so I just started flailing in the water. Without hesitation, my Dad jumped in to save me – wallet in his pockets and all. The club quickly found out that Mindee couldn't swim so they started putting me in the end lane just in case my Dad had to jump in to save me again. On the occasion that I completed an entire lap, I would look up to find everyone already getting out of the pool. I was always dead last. I know this chapter establishes the rejection in my life, but I feel like you need a win as the reader! Here's a quick one. It happened at the championship meet, of all places! The meet was hosted at a local college which had a heated, indoor pool. Who knew that could make such a huge difference. When I dove into the pool, the water felt amazing! I got to the business of swimming my heart out right away. As I drew closer to the end of the lane, I could see everyone screaming with every breath I took as I lifted and turned my head to the side. It wasn't until I got to the end that I realized I had won my heat! To this day, I am still very proud of that ribbon!

There's my win! And just like that, we're back from our commercial break! The previous memory of my Dad diving in to save me was always in the back of my mind. I knew that my Dad would always be there to rescue me whenever life got over my head. As unsettling as it is to consider, whenever he would tell me I was beautiful or would hug me, I would always have this uncomfortable feeling. I just couldn't figure out why. He had never been inappropriate with me in any way and acted as a loving father would all the time! I had so much confusion with that for so long. The other important piece I know now is that older men in power scared me because that's what Micah had been to me at the time that he violated me.

As a result, I feared older men in power no matter who it was. Despite this, I really wanted to strengthen my relationship with my Heavenly Father at the beginning of my senior year of high school. I figured God wasn't giving me my desires to have a boyfriend because I wasn't close enough to Him so I decided to fix that. I told my mentor I was going to abandon chasing and dating boys in favor of chasing after God. And of course, wouldn't you know it... that was when I met

Jason (not to be confused with Jason from fifth grade)! He was new to our youth group and was very cute. He didn't go to my school, so I only saw him a couple times a week. This checked the long-distance box that I unknowingly had so we ended up getting into a relationship. Right out of the gate, this relationship was different. I knew it was different, but I didn't quite know why or how. Looking back, I can see that it was because he respected me as a woman of God and sister in Christ. We even discussed making sure we put God as the center of our relationship. And honestly, I don't think I ever really considered what that could look like for me.

Even so, I still had major insecurities, which made me wonder why he stayed with me. Perhaps God was showing me what acceptance looks like on earth so that I could begin to envision and receive it from heaven. All I knew at the time was that I was comfortable with him which was something very new to me. We had our intimate moments when we would kiss, but he never once touched me in an inappropriate way. There was a small part of me that associated inappropriate touching with a man liking me which I struggled with from time to time. Did that mean he didn't really like me or that he was just being the gentleman I deserved as a daughter of the King? The bigger part of me focused on the words he spoke to me as the main like factor, though. He truly was a gentleman – probably the first gentleman I had ever dated.

This should come as no surprise but something still felt off. We had been dating a few months when we both went on a retreat with our youth group. It was that little window right after Christmas but before New Year's. I kept getting the feeling that something was wrong. My mentor Jill was at the retreat, so I sat with her to talk about it. All I could think about was that I broke that commitment to stop dating so I could grow closer to God in my last year of high school. I knew what I had to do… I just didn't want to do it. Through many tears, I broke up with Jason right there on the spot. Looking back, I should have waited until the end of the retreat because we both were miserable the rest of the time we were there.

To this day, I don't feel like I completely pinpointed what that off feeling was, but I will never forget how I broke his heart. My heart was broken, too. He told me that I had hurt him more than anyone else in his life. That was the first time I had ever experienced hurting someone and myself at the same time to that degree. It felt awful. I had many conflicting feelings going on inside me going into the new year. Over the next few years, I tried getting back together with him a few times. After a few years, we actually became friends again and hung out a lot platonically. It felt like we got close to getting back together once, but it never happened. Unfortunately, I don't think he ever fully trusted me with his heart again. I think the reason I kept going back to him was because there was a part of me that felt so safe with him. He really cared about me more than any other guy could have to that point. He was an amazing Christian man who consistently treated me how I ought to be treated. Perhaps he restored in me what Micah had ruined: the concept of a true Christian man. The finality of our relationship came when he got engaged to someone else. It crushed me. Those dark passengers just kept piling in; telling me I wasn't worth it and that I'd never find another guy who was ever going to really care about me like that again.

Journal Thoughts:

- What makes you feel fear? Write a few examples.

- What makes you feel rejection? Write a few examples.

- Have you ever experienced something that should be good, but because of your fears, you treated it as something bad?

- Take the examples mentioned above and write how they would have been different if you believed the truth of what God says about you in:

Psalm 139:14	1 John 4:4
1 Corinthians 6:11b	Romans 1:7
2 Corinthians 5:17	Ephesians 2:4
Ephesians 1:7-9	Colossians 3:12

JOURNAL YOUR JOURNEY

CONFESSIONS & FORGIVENESS

I spent a lot of time with my mentor Jill the summer after my senior year of high school. She spent much of that time keeping it real with me; mainly, by challenging me to go my first semester in college without dating anyone. Not even so much as a kiss. This was a huge challenge for me because that is the only thing that made me feel good about myself; but I accepted it. I went into my freshman year of college recommitted to concentrating on my relationship with God and God only.

As I said in the introduction, I went to Indiana Wesleyan University (IWU) in Marion, Indiana. I chose IWU because I had an uncle who was a professor there. Another deciding factor was due to my brother Randy's attendance there, as well. Not to mention a friend of my younger cousin Josh lived in the area, as well: Miriam. Miriam (whose mother was the professor of my psychology class) would become a precious friend to me. The summer heading into my first year in college, she encouraged me greatly with letters containing scriptures and devotional thoughts. Even though she wouldn't be around campus all the time, I was really excited to have her friendship close by. Such familiarity made IWU feel close enough to being a home away from home. However, if I'm being honest, the main draw for me to go to an out-of-state college right next door to Ohio was a fresh start. A do-over or mulligan, if you will. Other than a few of my brother's friends, I didn't really know anyone. No one from my high school went there which meant no one could remind me of my past mistakes, intentionally or otherwise.

Like a typical freshman, I had no clue what I wanted to do with my life. When it came time to choose a major, I spent time talking it through with my Aunt Cindy. She asked me what things I enjoyed doing the most. I told her I just wanted to get married and have a family. She jokingly said I would have to choose a major to go along with my MRS. degree. After a few laughs, I told her I enjoyed writing, singing and drama which led her to suggesting a communication degree. With a little further investigation, that seemed like the most natural thing to do; so that's what I declared my major to be.

As it turned out, I would be introduced to a close friend of Aunt Cindy's who would cause me to focus more on psychology. Dr. Betty Jane "BJ" Fratzke, who also happened to be friends with my uncle who taught at IWU, became my psychology professor. At this point in my life, I had no interest in psychology; however, Dr. Fratzke being Miriam's mother would grant her extra access to me. I honestly had never even thought about it. Simply put, psychology is basically the study of human behavior.

There have been many important people over the centuries who have studied and provided significant contributions on the subject of human behavior. Some of the popular ones being Sigmund Freud and Erik Erikson. Some of their theories were pretty crazy, while others... made sense.

Thanks to my uncle's guidance, I chose Dr. Fratzke's psychology class as an elective. The class took off fast. We were only a few lessons in when she started talking about Freud and Erikson's theories. Each had very different perspectives; but my feeling is that there are aspects within them that can be true depending on the person and the situation. Knowing this, there are various ways of counseling a person. Don't worry - I won't bore you with the details of them all! Just know that what I learned opened my eyes in ways I had never known it was possible to see. As I sat in class those first few days, I started to hear things that, though they scared me, gave me hope at the same time. For the first time in my life, I heard that traumatic things that happen to you as a child can cause your mind to act in different ways as you mature. I heard that when exposed to sexual abuse at an early age, children can become fearful and untrusting in relationships as they grow up. If I could take one whole page of this book, I would write in big capital letters: "WHAT?!?!?!" Even so, it still wouldn't do justice to the revelation I had in that moment. You know that light bulb moment people have from time to time? Well, mine was like the sun coming out after 12 long years of darkness!

For a few days after my big revelation, I wasn't sure what to do. Do I just keep it all inside and deal with all my dark passengers or do I tell someone and try to find some treatment? Is there any hope for me to be healed and whole or will I have to learn to manage this for the rest of my natural life? These were important questions I couldn't answer on my own so I decided to call Miriam to ask if I could meet with her and her mom to talk to finally begin figuring this out. After checking all three of our calendars, we agreed to meet one afternoon in Dr. Fratzke's office. Miriam, her mother and I sat in a small circle in front of her desk. Her office was what you would expect a therapist's office to look and feel like. Though it was comfortable, all I could hear was my heart beating out of my chest as my rising anxiety caused my muscles to tense. What had I gotten myself into now?!!

I knew what my trauma had been. It wasn't like it was suppressed enough that my professor would have to dig it out. The real question to answer was: How do I start? I really struggled to come up with the right words. If I spoke it out loud, it would be out there for what felt like the world to see. Even though it was only two people, it might hurt really bad for them to see all of who I was. Once I said the words, there was no turning back. They would know my darkest secret. How do I say the words and survive what they will think of me? How do I say the words and survive losing everyone I love because of what I did? How do I say the words and survive no one ever being able to love me? Once I released those words, they might find their way to my parents… and I didn't want them to know! My Dad would want to save me again, but he wouldn't be able to. The damage had already been done. What if he went to go find Micah and killed him for what he had done to his baby girl? Can I survive saying the words?

Even worse, can I survive if I don't say the words? Can I live the rest of my life hating myself? Can I live feeling afraid of people who want to love me? Can I live with being frozen at the touch of a loved one? Can I live with the pain building inside of me? Can I live with being afraid of someone loving me? Can I live with basing my identity in what I think others think of me? Can I live believing that I am as ugly as the pain I feel? Can I continue living with the weight of these dark passengers?

There was only one way to find out. As I opened my mouth, I begged God to give me the strength. I don't even remember what I said or how I said it, but I know that as I was talking, it felt like a boulder fell off my shoulders. I named it:

"I was sexually abused!"

I let it out. And I've got to tell you – I felt such freedom naming it! I had no clue how much holding on to a secret like that could weigh a person down! I sobbed as the words flowed past my lips to recount my story. As I finished retelling what happened to me, I could feel my dark passengers begin to rise up. Miriam and BJ will surely want nothing to do with me now. I should just get up and walk out before I die of embarrassment!

But before those thoughts could take over, their actions intervened. More than anything else in that moment, I felt loved and accepted. I was told repeatedly that it was not my fault. They affirmed me. I was told that my life didn't have to stay this way. Though it would take time, I was told that healing would come and they were there to help and support me.

This was not at all what my dark passengers had convinced me to expect. Was it what I was hoping for in the back of my mind? Absolutely! I just didn't really believe I could ever receive such acceptance and love. Now I had work to do. I needed to begin to accept and love myself. I knew it was going to be a long road; but it was a road I was willing to travel because I was tired of all these negative thoughts coming towards me from within. Just like I'd snapped a long losing streak at my swim meets, it was time for their winning streak to come to an end… permanently. I was done with them eating away at my soul and taking control of my life. I was done with death looming over my shoulders.

After this watershed moment, I began meeting with Dr. Fratzke weekly. First, we started with a few major things that I needed to improve on: self-esteem and self-love. Both had been greatly damaged throughout my adolescence to early adulthood. Next, I needed to address being uncomfortable around my Dad. Lastly, I needed to learn how to forgive Micah. While I'm sure the first two seem normal and necessary, I'm sure you may be thinking: "How do you forgive someone who could hurt a child so badly?" In truth, this was not the order I operated in; the first thing I worked on doing was the last thing most people are willing to do. You know the scripture that says the first shall be last and the last shall be first, right? Well, the first thing I actually worked on was forgiving Micah.

Why, you ask? Well, I thought back to one of my Bible classes in high school when we had discussed what bitterness and resentment can do to your body. They can wreak havoc on your system and cause all kinds of issues. Have you ever seen a person who is really bitter and angry at someone or the world, in general? They are never happy and everything in their life seems miserable. They always seem to have something wrong with them whether it's chronic sickness (such as colds, flus or complications with their organs), headaches and even cancer. I once heard that bitterness is like drinking poison and expecting the other person to die. Without a doubt, its impact manifests in our bodies like ingested venom. From a spiritual perspective, unforgiveness opens the door to bitterness which then leaves a gaping double door open for other dark passengers to enter your life.

My other motivation for forgiving Micah stemmed from my desire to please God by doing what He wanted me to do. Matthew 6:14-15 says:

> "For if you forgive other people when they sin against you, your heavenly Father will also forgive you. But if you do not forgive others their sins, your Father will not forgive your sins." (NIV)

I began feeling like God would give me the desires of my heart (someone to love and care for me) if I did all the things that He asked me to do. This may not sound like a bad thing, but it was a very destructive thought process that caused even more problems for many years to come. Flawed as it was, this approach helped me tremendously because forgiving Micah was more for my benefit than it was for him. I didn't want Micah to take up any more space in my mind than he already had because that space was giving him a lot of power over me. Forgiving him helped me to let go so I could work on restoring my true identity.

Though I had fleeting thoughts of seeking revenge on Micah, I was driven to confront him more so because of my biggest fear that he was still doing this to other girls. The dilemma in confronting him was that I'd heard he had become a youth pastor. What if he was no longer such a bad person and predator? Maybe… just maybe he had repented from abusing children and he was a safe person. Though I didn't want to destroy the person he might have become, I was haunted and overwhelmed by the likelihood that he was still sexually abusing children. It had been too long since the abuse had happened for me to go to the police. Besides, I had no way of knowing where he even was. I knew the city he was supposedly in, but the internet was brand new and you couldn't just look up a person on the computer. Once I found what could have been his address, I decided to write him a letter.

I wanted so many things out of this letter. In this letter, I wanted him to know that I remembered everything he had done to me. I wanted him to know that despite years of trauma, I was going to be okay. I wanted him to know how I prayed to God that he was a different person and that I prayed for the strength to forgive him. It was important for me to send this letter. I prayed for hours over that letter and I asked God that if this was something Micah needed to get, that it would find its way to him. I also prayed that if it was something he didn't need but that I really needed for closure, then to let it find its way to the bottom of a pile somewhere. To this day, I still don't know which of those happened. Either way, it helped me to let it go and truly forgive him.

Journal Thoughts:

- Have you named what happened to you yet? Not just in your mind, but out loud to a trusted person. If so, how and what did you feel? If not, what's holding you back?

- Have you forgiven the person or people who hurt you? If so, how did that feel? Do you find yourself having to forgive that person over and over again? If you've yet to forgive your violator(s), do you know the reason why? What needs to happen before you can forgive? Do you feel like forgiveness is more about you or them?

JOURNAL YOUR JOURNEY

THE BIG PICTURE IS HARD WORK

Working on myself took time. It's hard to change everything I thought about myself for all those years. In that time, I told my mentor Jill about what had happened to me. I think her eyes were opened to a better understanding of who I was in high school. She really encouraged me to tell my parents but that was going to take me a little longer.

In my counseling with Dr. Fratzke, I did a lot of what they call cognitive therapy. Basically, cognitive therapy is using thoughts, emotions and feelings to help correct the negative, inaccurate thinking and behaviors we have. It isn't really something that happens overnight. I used a lot of scripture affirmations to try and see myself how God sees me. I would look in the mirror and repeat these lines:

- I have a future and a hope. (Jeremiah 29:11)
- My life is restored. (Psalm 71:20)
- I am wonderfully made. (Psalm 139:14)
- I am loved. (Jeremiah 31:3)
- I am chosen. (John 15:16)
- I am God's child (Romans 8:17)
- Nothing can separate me from God's love. (Romans 8:35)
- I am accepted. (Romans 15:7)

- I am a new creation. (2 Corinthians 5:17)
- I am blameless in Christ. (Ephesians 1:4)
- I am strong. (Ephesians 6:10)
- I am chosen and deeply loved. (Colossians 3:12)
- God will meet all my needs. (Philippians 4:19)
- I am never alone. (Hebrews 13:5)
- I am forgiven. (1 John 2:12)

Saying these things to myself wasn't always the easiest thing to do and they may prove difficult for you, as well. However, when you speak God's truths to yourself, you will eventually start to believe them as I did.

Can I ask you an honest question? Did you actually take the time to read through those scriptures beyond the Cliff Notes I just provided?!! Did you journey through them (take some time to reflect on them as you walked back through your pain) and say them out loud to yourself? If not, please take some time to do that now. It will be well worth your while – I promise! I'll wait... Now that you've done that, let's look at some typical symptoms people have that are smaller pieces of a bigger picture.

Anger

Though anger is a natural stage of grief, we shouldn't stay in it for very long. Yet, this is normally not the case. Many people deny or suppress their anger - causing them to fester in it unknowingly until something large or small triggers it to the surface. Many people feel anger in multiple directions when it comes to abuse.

Personally speaking, I felt a lot of anger towards myself. It's not uncommon for people to feel anger towards God, as well. Common questions are:

- God, why did You allow this to happen to me?
- God, why did You allow this to happen to someone I love?

There's a lot we don't understand about why things happen in this world. Many of them are scary. Most people don't like being scared without a way to disarm it which is why anger is such a common response. The worst-case scenario for people carrying around anger towards God is that they both blame and begin to question Who He is. Ultimately, this can cause a person to stop following and believing in Him altogether.

What we need to understand is that we live in a fallen world that God left in our care. We have the mandate and power to restore order to the world through Jesus and the Holy Spirit. We also have the free will to make our own choices: some are good, some are bad, some are downright horrible. We can't blame God for our choices or anyone else's choices. Another painful question at the center of the abandonment people feel towards God is:

- God, where were You when the abuse happened?

This may be hard to read but He was right there with me and with you. He was just as broken-hearted and violated. He wept for us. While He hated what He was seeing, His interfering would compromise our freedom as well as prevent us from ultimately having a place of vulnerability to minister from for others who are abused. This is where Genesis 50:20 comes to life:

> "You intended to harm me, but God intended it for good to accomplish what is now being done, the saving of many lives."

Recalling the story, Joseph spoke this to his brothers after realizing that everything they had wrongfully done to him only positioned him to ultimately save their entire lineage once he became a high-ranking official in Egypt during an historic famine. He oversaw the provisions that his brothers came to Egypt to receive. Provisions that Egypt itself wouldn't have had if they hadn't sold him into slavery.

In similar fashion, Satan meant this abuse to harm and destroy me, but God is using it for good. This book is meant to fill a void needed for an entire teenage demographic grappling with the aftermath of being sexually abused. But in order for this book to come to pass, I had to accept what happened to me, stop finding blame in others, forgive my abuser and realize that I have something valuable to contribute to the world despite and because of what I've managed to survive. I could've kept this story to myself once I received my deliverance. The choice of one person (me) being set free versus scores and scores of people being delivered was up to me. This outcome was mine to decide. I made the decision that I wasn't going to let Satan get the victory for this. I was going to allow God to have the glory and victory by helping as many people as I can.

S.S.S.: Shame, Self-Harm and Surfing

Much of the shame I experienced was internal during my formative years. These days, there is a new element that amplifies it beyond belief – causing the number of suicides to skyrocket in the current generation of millennials: social media. When the internet first broke, we had a name for spending hours on end exploring every corner of the world which it brought to our fingertips: surfing. I'm not sure if it's still called this but it's fitting in that people are literally wiping out and drowning as everyone watches it unfold in real time. As people cope with their loneliness, they're letting it play out in front of audiences now more than ever which opens the door to cyber bullying. Some of the assault is even captured live as guys are preying on girls (and vice versa) who are desperate enough for attention to record getting drunk or high for the sake of going viral. When it goes awry (which it often does) the attention they were seeking takes a turn for the worse as the shaming gets magnified by the very audience – largely composed of strangers – they were seeking acceptance and approval from in the first place. While I was able to hide my trauma and avoid a platform with such a public and instant reaction, those wanting to be influencers are often ill-equipped to handle the reading through the backlash of horrifically cruel comments telling them they're "easy" or calling them "sluts."

As if the petty name-calling wasn't bad enough, they're also fed the lie that they got what they deserved for their bad decision. The fault gets placed on the victim rather than the victimizer. I've read that it's gone so far, that entire families have had to move out of state because of the harassment. That may have been effective in my day, but you can't outrun the internet. Sure, you can delete your account but anything that's electronic can be downloaded and brought back up in your face as people prone to stalking tendencies have free reign on the various platforms that presently exist. While suicide has already been discussed, non-fatal self-harm is on the rise as a coping mechanism, as well.

If this has hit close to home, I beg you, please hear what I am saying. I don't care what indiscretion it was: getting drunk, getting high, sexual experimentation, etc. No one, and I mean NO ONE, has the right to sexually assault you. That was their choice and it is not your fault! You are not defined by what others think of you!! You are every one of those affirmations written at the beginning of this chapter. Those lies that others think and say are from the enemy and are meant to pull you down. They're meant to cause you harm. Let God's truth penetrate your heart and your fight! Fight for yourself! Fight for others! Proverbs 23:7a (AMP) says:

"For as he thinks in his heart, so is he…"

Fight for your identity to be who God says you are. If you believe it in your heart, then you will be able to live it out. Don't let the enemy win!

Manipulation/Control

Another thing that is typical in someone who's been abused is an overwhelming need to control people and situations around them. Once that control exerts itself on someone else's free will, it becomes manipulation. In fact, it is a direct response to the manipulation that accompanies the original abuse. Micah manipulated myself and my friend by lying about his true intentions in order to force his will on us. I didn't have control when I was being abused and, as I grew older, I made sure to never let it happen again... by any means necessary. I didn't feel as though I was being malicious in my desire to control others around me; I just wanted to take back what was taken from me: my safety and the right to choose my outcomes with full knowledge of what was being done to me.

When this is your driving motivation, you'll find yourself on a mission to control as much of your life as possible before you know it. Your weight is something you can control; so maybe you like controlling your body which leads to an eating disorder like bulimia or anorexia. The sad part of this is that if it spirals out of control, an eating disorder will eventually control you. There's enough complexity in this topic alone that demands another book entirely. However, for the time being, if this is something you struggle with – please seek help. As much as you think you have control over it, you can't fight it alone.

At the other end of the spectrum, you may overeat to

the extent that you gain weight. It's been found that the rationale behind teenagers who overeat stems from the belief that if they gain weight, the abuser will stop because they're no longer attracted to them. Unfortunately, this is yet another lie the enemy uses so that he can take control of your life. Much like overeating to comfort oneself as a coping mechanism, you'll end up addicted to food; fighting a losing battle where it controls you more than you control it.

My issues with control presented themselves a little bit differently. When I found myself in a situation where it wasn't possible for me to have control, I would become overly anxious. My youngest brother Brett was born when I was fifteen. I spent a lot of time with him while he was growing up which means we developed a very special bond. When Brett was twelve, our family took a trip to Disneyworld. We all decided to ride Space Mountain. For those who have never been on this ride, the whole thing is in the dark to mimic being in outer space. The seats are individual with a person in front of you and behind you. Brett sat behind me and I panicked the entire ride because I couldn't sit next to him. What if the mechanical arm that kept him in his seat came undone and he fell out? No one would ever know, and he could die. If only I was sitting next to him, I could protect him. That's what was going through my mind. Needless to say, I was miserable because I couldn't control the situation playing out in my head! I wasn't even afraid of falling out myself. I was afraid of not being there for him. I couldn't control what was happening and it made me sick. I had the same reaction when trying to ride a horse or trying to sleep when someone else was driving. The less control I had, the higher anxiety I felt.

I still struggle with controlling certain things. It's exhausting! For example, my husband loves chocolate chip cookies – in small part, because I've finally perfected the recipe. If he tells me he is going to make them himself, though? In my mind, I'm the only one who can make them perfectly. This is how it is with most things in my life: nothing will be done correctly unless I do them. Even if that means I end up doing everything, so be it! Whether it's party planning, baking, cooking, projects (work or school), etc. Though the thing I'm controlling may turn out exactly how I like it, I find myself exhausted from doing it all myself or alone because I've alienated everyone from helping.

Though it's easier said than done, letting other people in is the best way to let go of control. I've gotten better but I still have work to do. Besides, you never know. We just may find out someone else has a better way or can actually do something better than us! I know – it's risky but that's okay! It's worth the risk to ensure that you're neither boxing yourself in or boxing others out.

Fear

One of the things we discovered in counseling was the fear that I had at even the thought of seeing Micah again. That was something I couldn't control, so this particular dark passenger would take over whenever the possibility of running into him entered my thoughts. At the time I discovered this, I hadn't seen him in years. I didn't even know if there would ever be an occasion where I would see him again. But because there was always that chance, I felt like I needed to prepare myself more; but I was never prepared enough. The best preparation I could provide myself was to push past the fear. 2 Timothy 1:7 says:

> "For God gave us a spirit **NOT** of fear but of power and love and self-control."
> (ESV, emphasis added)

Fear has nothing to do with God. If there's ever a time when you feel fear, send it right back where it came from because it's from the enemy who is doing all he can to destroy you. It didn't happen overnight, but I got to the point where I could see how holding on to the fear and anger was only hurting me; it did absolutely nothing to Micah. Why would I let him get away with making me miserable (see Proverbs 10:12)? I was finally able to believe he couldn't hurt me anymore through a lot of prayer, time and work.

At this point in my story, I want to emphasize the importance of seeking out a licensed counselor to help you or your loved one learn how to cope with what has happened and how to move forward. Though my purpose is to give you hope and understanding, a counselor can help bring healing beyond what this book can do. If you don't know a counselor, then ask a pastor or trusted friend to help you find a good one in your area.

Being able to talk about what happened made me feel

so much better. In fact, there were times when all I could do was talk about it. Whenever I saw my mentor Jill, it dominated the topic of conversation. Eventually, I got to the point where I felt ready to tell my parents. I knew how much my parents loved me, and my biggest fear was that this would hurt them because of the pain it caused me. When I sat with them, the fear wasn't as big as when I first told Dr. Fratzke and Miriam, but I was still nervous. My parents were sad for me, but their love and compassion helped the healing process continue. Initially, I didn't reveal the name of the abuser until my Dad promised he wouldn't kill him. Though he did promise not to kill Micah, he said all I had to do was give him the word and he would. Thankfully, I never put that hit on Micah. Lord knows we didn't need to complicate matters with my Dad (or my brothers) trying to beat a murder charge! My family has been nothing but supportive of me through this whole process and again I say, I know I am blessed!

Though I went into details of a few symptoms stemming from sexual abuse, I'd like to highlight some others that may be plaguing you. Some of these symptoms I have had, others I have not. It's quite typical not to see all of these in one person. If you do see one or a few of them, then it's very possible that person has suffered sexual abuse and trauma before the age of 18. Please be aware that this is not meant to be an exhaustive list as taken from the American Academy of Experts in Traumatic Stress:

- Withdrawal and mistrust of adults

- Suicidality
- Difficulty relating to others except in sexual or seductive ways
- Unusual interest in or avoidance of all things sexual or physical
- Sleep problems, nightmares, fears of going to bed
- Frequent accidents or self-injurious behaviors
- Refusal to go to out
- Secretiveness or unusual aggressiveness
- Sexually-themed drawings or games
- Neurotic reactions (obsessions, phobias, compulsiveness)
- Habit disorders (biting, rocking)
- Unusual sexual knowledge or behavior
- Prostitution
- Forcing sexual acts on other children
- Extreme fear of being touched
- Unwillingness to submit to physical examinations

You may be experiencing some of these and not even realize where it came from or why. I certainly didn't understand the ones I experienced growing up. I questioned many times why I dealt with some of these things, but I never sought answers because of the shame that came with them. As I started working through them, I had a lot of clarity, but it still took time. At that point, my identity was so wrapped up in what people thought of me. Rejection was something I felt every day. It had almost become a pair of glasses I put on, and everything I experienced was filtered through that rejection. If someone looked at me and snarled their nose up and squinted their eyes, I automatically thought they must think I am pretty ugly. When in actuality, they may have just crossed paths with someone who passed gas. I always turned everything someone said or did into something negative towards myself. This is a hard thing to let go of and sometimes we pick that rejection back up. Even today I sometimes let that dark passenger find its way in and struggle with the same issue.

I'm not saying all this to make you feel like things will always be hard. I say these things because you need to understand it takes a lot more than just changing your mind to change your heart. You also need to understand that you have a quicker chance of recovery if you have a supportive, caring adult to walk with you through your recovery. I had so many people in my life to fill this role. If they had only known what I had gone through, they would've been right there at my side to walk through it all in a heartbeat.

Though I had an amazing breakthrough thanks to these counseling sessions, I stopped going because I wound up moving back to Ohio after the first semester of my sophomore year. Without that consistent level of counseling, it didn't take long before my dark passengers began presenting themselves again just as the Bible tells us in Luke 11:24-26 (ESV):

> "When the unclean spirit has gone out of a person, it passes through waterless places seeking rest, and finding none it says, 'I will return to my house from which I came.' And when it comes, it finds the house swept and put in order. Then it goes and brings seven other spirits more evil than itself, and they enter and dwell there. And the last state of that person is worse than the first."

Hence, the rest of my story.

Journal Thoughts:

- Try looking in a mirror and saying the scripture affirmations from the beginning of this chapter. How do they make you feel? Start memorizing some of the scripture affirmations so that when you start to feel a dark passenger rise up, you can fight it off with the word of God as a double-edged sword (see Hebrews 4:12, Ephesians 6:17)!

- Do any of the symptoms of sexual abuse fit you? Name them and write about your experiences. Next, talk to a trusted adult or counselor about them so you can make a plan to find healing from them.

JOURNAL YOUR JOURNEY

THE "RESET" OF MY STORY

The summer after my freshman year of college was very different than when I was in high school. When I came back home, most of my high school friends were off doing new things. My church had a college and career group, but I only knew one person from my group of high school friends: Caitlin. She invited me to come hang out with some people from the group. I don't think I can recapture what happened better than my journal entry from May 9, 1995:

> *"Well, I have been out of school for two weeks and here I am back in Ohio. I will be coaching Lakeview High School cheerleading, so I had to come back for their tryouts. I am so depressed. Sunday night I met this guy. His name is Anthony, but I get to call him Tony. He was visiting from Oregon. This is how I met him. Sunday night I decided to go to church. I went by myself and figured I would just find someone to sit with. When I walked in, I saw Caitlin and she asked me to sit*

with her and I sat on the end of the row. She got up to go to the bathroom and when she came back there were two guys with her. One of them I recognized as Paul, a guy in our college group. I didn't recognize the other guy, but he sure was cute! At first, I didn't really think much of it. After church Caitlin asked me if I wanted to go out with the college group. I agreed and went outside to meet them. I only knew two of the twelve people out there, so I just stood by Caitlin. We were all just talking when that cute guy came and stood beside me. He turned to me, stuck out his hand and said, 'What's your name?' I said 'Mindee' and he said 'Hi Mindee I am Anthony.' I got a little nervous so I turned around and started talking to Caitlin. Then they decided to go to Rocky's Pizza. I got to know Anthony a little better there. On the way out I put a quarter in one of those toy machines and I got this pink bracelet. I put it on and was joking about my new bracelet. They all decided to go to Tyler's and play games. It was getting late and people were leaving, but Tony wanted to keep hanging out. Everyone had work or school in the morning except Tony, Paul, and I. The three of us decided to go to Denny's by the mall. It was about 12:15 when we got there, and I just got some iced tea while they got food. About 2:30 or 3:00 Paul left, and Tony and I talked about everything! We know each other so well. I feel like I have known him all my life. He really looks like a young Jean-Claude Van Damme! He is 5'7" and so sweet! He is a good Christian and the perfect guy. Except he lives all the way across the country. We sat there and faced each other, and he put his hand on my knee. Every once in a while, he would hold my hand. We left around 5:15 am and in the parking lot he came up to me, hugged me, and kissed me on the cheek. Then we said goodbye."

Tony and I spent the entire summer writing back and

forth. There were times I would get multiple letters in one day! We also talked on the phone when we could, but back then we had to pay for long distance phone calls, so it got expensive. He was the first guy to ever have flowers delivered to me with notes telling me how beautiful I was. This continued for months. Here was a guy who continued to tell me how much he cared for me and how much he liked me without physical contact. This sounds like the perfect situation for me, doesn't it?!! Only my insecurity began to creep in. Could a guy really like me without a physical relationship? It caused me to question if he meant what he said about me. Was he getting the physical intimacy that men stereotypically needed from someone else? There went my heart.

I had to find out so I could put this paranoia to bed. It just so happened that Caitlin's mom lived on the west coast like Tony. Further still, she just so happened to live in the same city as Tony, too! You know what that meant, right? ROAD TRIP! So, the weekend before I was supposed to start my sophomore year at IWU, we decided to go on a girls' trip to the West coast. Tony met me with roses and a lot of fun plans for the weekend the minute I got off the plane (clearly, this was before 9/11). Every day, he would pick me up and take me on some amazing adventure. I had borscht for the first time. He even made me dinner one evening and, to my surprise, both were delicious! We did so much together that most might consider ordinary. We walked around town. We talked a lot. We watched movies and played games at the arcade together. These were simple pleasures, but they meant the world to me.

One day, we went hiking. One thing that separates the West from the Ohio plains are the mountains. Not just mountains but majestic, snow-capped mountains. It was so beautiful! On the last leg of our hike, we ferried to an island where, to my shock, we ended up talking about the possibility of marriage in our future. The excitement I felt in that moment was almost electric, but it was immediately grounded by this weird feeling.

> "He couldn't want to marry me. That would mean he loved me. He couldn't possibly feel that way."

These words kept ringing on repeat in my head. Up to this point in my life, no one had ever felt that way about me enough to actually express it out loud. The closest thing to such an expression had only been something written down – never before had it been spoken out loud. I couldn't wrap my mind around it, so I pushed the reality of it away as we continued on with our fun day.

After hiking, Tony dropped me back off at Caitlin's mom's house to clean up. Our day was far from over because Tony had plans to take me to a nice restaurant. Remember, sweaty and hot Mindee?!! I definitely needed time to freshen up to get ready for our evening. I wore a black cocktail dress which he complemented well with a nice suit and tie. Mom and Dad would've been impressed with his ability to dress for the occasion unlike my Homecoming date back in the day!

I wanted to feel as beautiful as I could so I did not leave anything to chance. That's why I let Caitlin help me with my hair and makeup. Between her skills and Tony doing everything he could to make me feel beautiful and tended to, I suppose I did have a moment when I felt special. Even so, I still couldn't allow myself to fully believe it. When he came to pick me up, we took pictures and he brought me another rose. It was the beginning of a magical evening.

We arrived at the restaurant and it was perfect. Like, Hallmark movie perfect. I was sitting across from a handsome man who was treating me in a way I had never been treated. You could hear the crystal glasses clinking and the hushed conversations going on around us. There was even piano music playing in the background. It all happened in such a way that it felt as if I were watching someone else's life play out on screen. Then, it all crystallized in a moment. With three small words, I was drawn into the life that was playing out in front of me. But not just any life. This was my life! I'll never forget it as long as I live. Time seemed to slow down as Tony mouthed the words: "I love you." He didn't audibly say them but it was the closest I'd ever come to another man saying that phrase to me outside of my father and brothers. It wasn't platonic. It wasn't ironic. It was both romantic and honest. I felt like I had a tornado swirling in my chest. It was like my mind stopped working. The first time I ever had those words uttered to me and it played out like a romantic movie. Though it doesn't get much better than that, it sure got worse as my romantic chick flick turned into a full-blown comedy. One where I completely and utterly humiliated myself.

The first thing that popped into my adult head was an elementary school gag. Do you remember when kids would mouth the words "olive juice" because it looked like you were saying "I love you"? I thought I would just say that back to him in case that was what he was really doing. In case it wasn't fully clear before, my mind had stopped working. With my brain in a fog, I started mouthing "watermelon." Why "watermelon," you ask? Though my brain had completely betrayed me, it still had a bit of logic lurking around. You see, when you don't know the words to a song, you mouth the word "watermelon" over and over again because it looks like you're still singing the correct thing. I'd heard it works in professional video shoots, too – so why not now? It took a few moments for me to get the oxygen back to my brain but by then, the moment had passed; leaving me to look like a huge fool while making Tony feel like a fool, as well.

And just like that, Mindee had struck again! I began looking for any and every reason why he couldn't have possibly meant what it looked like he said. Did I really even know and understand what love was? I even brought the Bible into it. I knew what 1 Corinthians 13 said about love; specifically verses 4-7:

> "Love is patient and kind; love does not envy or boast; it is not arrogant or rude. It does not insist on its own way; it is not irritable or resentful; it does not rejoice at wrongdoing but rejoices with the truth. Love bears all things,

> believes all things, hopes all things, endures all things." (ESV)

Was it even possible for me to see that type of love outside of my family? Maybe with the people at church... but in a relationship? Though I really cared about Tony, I just didn't know if the love he had expressed to me was the same type of forever love that Paul wrote about to the people of Corinth. We were both in an immature time of our lives.

It probably comes as no surprise to you that my relationship with Tony didn't survive more than a few weeks after I came back from our trip. I really cared and thought about him often over the years, but I was incapable of getting to a place where I could really let him care about me; even though that was all my heart really wanted. I was leaving a trail of hurt men in the wake of my hurt. I was in a tailspin... and I felt absolutely powerless to stop it.

When I got back to IWU that Fall, I decided to just hang out with friends and have fun. By this time in my life, my friends were all the sports guys and the other cheerleaders. Have you ever heard the stereotype of jocks and cheerleaders?!! I'll just say this: groupthink is real! And just because you're in a group, doesn't mean you're always thinking! One night, we all decided to go play hide and go seek in a corn field (don't judge us... we were in Indiana, so there wasn't much else to do!). I simply needed to escape my own thoughts, so when the idea was suggested, I just went along for the ride. I didn't give it much thought until I stepped into that field. All of a sudden, fear decided to come along for the ride… and it completely took over. I was in a cornfield where all I could see was what the moonlight permitted me to view. The reality of me being alone in the dark of a cold night overpowered me. While everyone else was hiding from each other, I ran back to the car and waited. I was beyond relieved when everyone came back and decided to go to a friend's off-campus apartment. Though there were a lot of us, somehow, I ended up alone with a guy named Matt: the designated self-centered jerk of the group. I guess I had no one else to talk to because I don't remember why I was even sitting next to him.

The next thing I knew, he had grabbed my head and pushed it down to his crotch. The last time someone did that to me, I didn't know any better. Up to this point, I had always been the girl who was afraid to say "No" to anyone for fear of rejection. Even if a guy was trying to kiss me, I would just let him. I would close my eyes and bear it. This time was different. Not only did I say "No," I slammed my hands down, got up and walked out. I was so angry that a guy I didn't really know would have the nerve to think I would want to do something like that to him. Soon after, I reflected on that incident and wondered if the counseling had taken root because I hadn't been afraid to walk away from someone who wanted to use me for his pleasure. Were my dark passengers all gone? Had I just regained some healthy control?

Journal Thoughts:

- Do you have situations that seem to happen over and over in your life? Write at least one situation that you find yourself falling into repeatedly. What is one thing you can choose to do differently the next time you fall into it?

- Has there ever been a time when you have felt you had healing from something only to find you still struggle with it? Name it and write out how it makes you feel when it returns. Next, talk it through with a trusted adult or counselor.

JOURNAL YOUR JOURNEY

WRONG AGAIN

I ended up leaving IWU after the first semester of my sophomore year. I can't say how much of my decision was influenced by the night of the cornfield maze but it was largely because I really had no clue what I wanted to do. Plus, I was going into a lot of debt. It was a great school, but I figured it was wiser for me economically to earn an Associate's degree at a local community college. I went home thinking I had done enough counseling. After all, I stood up for myself against an aggressor for the first time which meant I was totally over sexual abuse. Wrong again.

Now that I was back home, I was able to pick up where I left off – spending much of my spare time with the college group at my church. We did a lot of fun stuff together. Between Bible studies, camping, white-water rafting and countless other activities, I had plenty of healthy distractions to keep my mind off my problems. I forged better friendships than the ones I had at IWU and we become a tight-knit group of friends with a shared commonality of nurturing our spiritual growth even though we were all in different places with our faith walk. Some were very mature, others not so much. Though I wasn't a baby, I knew I really needed to work towards strengthening my relationship with God. I felt comfortable with this group because they accepted me where I was and encouraged me along the way. I was thankful to have them in my life.

On one of our camping trips, our core group of friends fused with some new people. This was cool because all the "regulars" had gotten to know one another very well. One night, we were all sitting around the fire. I noticed that some of the new guys had brought beer. They offered me some, but I declined. I hate the taste of beer! As the evening went on, people began leaving one by one. After some more time had passed, this guy named Brad told me he wanted to show me something in his tent. He had been a little flirty with me all night, but I didn't think anything of it. I mean, why would I? We were on a Christian camping trip and with my church friends. I should have been safe. In hindsight, I should've been safe when I was six years old at my home church, but I didn't make that connection in the moment.

When I got to Brad's tent, I quickly discovered I wasn't so safe. He started kissing me. At first, I was shocked because I'd never even thought of him in that way. When I finally realized what was happening, I started pulling away as I told him to stop. From that point, everything went silent. It felt like everything I was trying to say wouldn't come out. Have you ever had a dream where you're trying to scream but nothing is coming out of your mouth? I managed to tell Brad "No" just like I had with Matt from the last chapter; and that should have been enough. Only this time, it wasn't. He kept going until he was on top of me. My heart was racing as I begged him to stop. Looking back, I can't even recall if my pleading was out loud or if it stayed in my mind. I did manage to utter "Slow down" – but it fell on deaf ears. The whole tent was spinning and all I could smell was the beer on his breath.

I wanted our friends to come in and stop him but the only ones who showed up were the dark passengers that I thought were long gone… and they were there having a party at my expense. To be clear, Brad did not rape me. He used my body to pleasure himself without my consent by forcing his hands and mouth all over me. This was still abuse and it had found a way into my life again. After what seemed like hours, he finally fell asleep with his arms on top of me. I was too afraid to even move. Why was I able to run away from Matt, but unable to stop Brad? The answer came in an instant. It was because I felt safe with Brad. I had let my guard down because I was in a safe place. I laid in the tent crying into the dark of night until the sun came up. I was nauseous. All I wanted to do was get out of his tent before anyone saw that I was in there. I didn't want anyone to think that I was in there willingly. Somehow, I mustered the strength to get up and go outside in time to throw up at a nearby tree. At that point, one of the other girls saw me and came over to see if I was alright. Instead of telling her what happened, the fear of being rejected and ridiculed showed up; so, I ended up telling her that I just wasn't feeling well. She walked away believing I would be fine, but I wouldn't.

I had play rehearsal with other members of our group that night once we got back from the camping grounds. One of the participants was Mike. He was really good friends with Brad. I was very close with Mike and, if I'm being honest, I had a little bit of a crush on him. I was so afraid of what Brad had told Mike. He came up to me after practice and asked me how I felt about Brad because he had heard we spent the night together. I broke down in tears and I told him everything that happened. I saw anger in his eyes. Was he angry at me because what he had heard was true? Was he blaming me as much as I was blaming myself? He looked at me, said, "He is a dead man!" and started to walk out. Though I felt relieved that he didn't blame me, I still ran after him and tried to stop him. Just like my Dad with Micah, I didn't want him to do anything that he would regret later. He said that he was going to make sure Brad made this right. There was no stopping him. I don't know what happened to this day, but Brad ended up calling and begging me to forgive him. He wanted to take me to dinner and talk, but I told him I didn't think it was a good idea. He asked me to at least let him take me for a drink after church. The fear of saying "No" returned; so, even though I didn't want to go, I agreed at his insistence.

Brad took me to Applebee's. It was the last place I wanted to be, but I felt I like had to go. It had more to do with the company than the restaurant. He apologized but then had the nerve to follow it up by asking if we could date! He actually sat there and said all the things most girls would love to hear but given the context, all it did was just make me want to throw up all over again. I told him that I needed time to think about it and I would let him know; but I already I knew inside that I would never be alone with him again.

Years went by with no steady relationships. If anything came close, it never lasted more than a few weeks.

I ended up becoming part of a church plant where I helped to start the youth group. I loved it. There were many times when I would see girls who reminded me of myself. I could even see their dark passengers. They looked an awful lot like mine. I would spend time with these young ladies and eventually find that they had all been abused in some way. I would encourage them as best I could until they were ready to tell their parents. From there, their parents were able to get them into counseling. Though having the ability to help these young girls in a way that no one else could was very fulfilling, in the back of mind I wanted more. I kept wondering:

> "If I was good enough, would God bring me my prince charming?"

If I just studied His Word enough, maybe… just maybe my perfect man would show up on my doorstep. Year after year, heartbreak after heartbreak, it was more of the same. What was wrong with me? I would journal over and over again asking God why no one wanted my heart – overlooking the fact that He was telling me He wanted my heart first.

One of those heartbreaks happened the summer I went on another camp outing with the youth – only I was one of the leaders responsible for their safety. One of the other leaders at this camp was a guy named Todd. The kids loved Todd. He was really outgoing. He was a good-looking guy, as well. For whatever reason, though there were plenty of other female camp leaders there, all the young girls thought he and I should hook up. Though it was neither appropriate as camp leaders or a good time for me to try anything like that, we did end up exchanging email addresses at the end of camp. We kept in touch. I went to visit a friend who attended the same college as Todd and ended up running into him. We decided to meet for coffee and ended up talking for five hours. There was nothing more to it besides two friends talking, but it was a lot of fun and I felt really encouraged. After that coincidental run-in, we moved from emailing one another to talking on the phone every now and then. He was a great help to me with the Bible study I was teaching the girls in youth group. Not that he was necessarily guiding me through the scriptures but more so by helping me model what it looks like to be with a guy with boundaries. You see, we were studying what relationships should look like. We spent a lot of time on how guys should treat girls and why staying as far away as possible from a physical relationship was the best thing they could do. I told him how important it was for me to be a good example. Besides, I had made a decision not to kiss another guy unless I knew we were in love.

A few months later, he asked if he could come visit me and some of the kids. We were taking the youth to a John Reuben concert who was one of Todd's favorite artists. It just so happened to be his birthday, so he looked at the event kind of like a birthday celebration. I totally trusted him because we were on the same page with our beliefs and values. I was living with a roommate at the time, so it wasn't appropriate for him to stay there. We decided we would both stay at my parents' house. Boundaries are a good thing, right?!! They had an extra bedroom in the basement that he could stay in while I stayed upstairs.

After the concert, we dropped some of the kids off at their homes and headed back to my parents' house. When we got there, I showed him where he would be sleeping. I also had a birthday present I gave him which he really appreciated. He gave me a hug and then kissed me on the cheek. I was a little taken back because I just didn't expect that to happen. I brushed it off as him being sweet and overwhelmed in the moment. We decided to go up to the living room to watch a movie. We sat on separate couches and I ended up falling asleep. All of a sudden, I woke up to Todd kissing my cheek again which made me sit up and push away from him very quickly. He sat next to me and pulled me into his arms. I was totally confused. At no point had he given any hint that he was interested in me. We sat there for a second before it abruptly ended by Todd saying that we should probably call it a night. I agreed. I was still a bit dazed as we got up and were walking down the hall. When we got to the steps where

I would go up and he would go down, he thanked me for the birthday present, leaned over and kissed my cheek again! I started to feel like this was a little more than a friendly thank you kiss. Before I knew it, he had grabbed me and started kissing me on the lips. I was trying to process in my mind when our relationship went from friends to… whatever he was forcing us into.

I started thinking about the girls in my group and how much of a hypocrite I was for teaching them to stay as far away from what I was now right smack in the middle of doing. I wanted him to stop, but when he didn't, I did. He apologized and basically admitted that though he was interested in me, he had too much going on in his life for a relationship.

At this point, I was beyond confused. Did he just give me the relationship bit to offset the advances he had started?!! Don't guys normally do that after they've slept with a girl and need to get out of being committed to them? Enough about Todd, though. I had been doing so good! I was beginning to feel so excited about my mental health. Now, all of the sudden, my dark passengers invaded my mind. All because someone I respected and trusted had made me feel like nothing more than a piece of meat presented to him on a plate for his pleasure. Doubt took over. It told me that not even a godly man could ever love me and desire me for the person I am inside. Maybe this was as good as I deserved.

Why would I say such a thing? Because the next night was a repeat of the first... only this time, Todd pushed it a lot further. I allowed it because he was the type of guy I wanted to love me. I had shared with him my kissing vow in some of the many talks we'd shared and he took advantage of it. I struggled with how to handle it all because though he was manipulating what he knew about me, I wanted him to love me. A part of me rationalized that he must feel the same way. Why else would he keep kissing on me so much? Different guy, same pattern. Before he left that weekend, he apologized just like Brad had; only no one had to threaten him to do it. It felt just as meaningless to me as Brad's apology, too. It wasn't long before Todd started ignoring my calls and then, just like that – my heart and mind were occupied by a stronghold of dark passengers.

Those dark passengers did their best to fill my mind with whatever was ugly, whatever was hurtful, whatever was fearful and whatever was wrong. But I refused to let them take over! I did my best to combat them with the Sword of the Spirit: the Word of God. Specifically, I countered and volleyed their strikes with Philippians 4:8:

> "Finally, brothers and sisters, whatever is true, whatever is noble, whatever is right, whatever is pure, whatever is lovely, whatever is admirable – if anything is excellent or praiseworthy – think about such things." (NIV)

The enemy's tactics distract us from the Word by getting us so caught up on ourselves that we lose sight of the weapon we have right at our fingertips. A weapon so powerful, it hits them hard enough to make them flee from our presence completely broken (see Deuteronomy 28:7). For all the damage it does to our spiritual enemy, in the same swipe, it can build us up:

> "For the word of God is living and active, sharper than any two-edged sword, piercing to the division of soul and of spirit, of joints and of

marrow, and discerning the thoughts and intentions of the heart." - Hebrews 4:12 (ESV)

Yet and still, we end up concentrating on the things that tear us down. Before Todd came, I was thinking of those good things Paul wrote to the Philippians. That's what had me in such a good place. The moment Todd took advantage of me, I lost sight of them all; allowing the enemy to regain a foothold. Clearly, I still wasn't confident enough in myself and who God created me to be. I was working as hard as I knew how to be loved by God and people, but I couldn't figure out what I was doing wrong. My problem was that I just kept trying to do it on my own.

It took a long time for me to get past what happened. I talked through it with my close friends who encouraged and loved me enough so that I was able to get back to loving and respecting myself again. I wound up seeing Todd one more time the next summer at camp. He only came for the first evening, but it was enough to stir up a lot of anxiety. Mostly because I didn't want to end up back in that same place. What was different this time was that I had backup! My best friend Kristi was there along with two of my close guy friends who knew what he had done to me. I was surrounded by love and friends who were very protective of me. They wouldn't let him come anywhere near me without my consent. He literally had to go through them just to speak to me. He claimed to have something important to tell me, so I gave them permission to let him through like the queen God made me to be!

With the limited time he had, he spent it telling me how God had been working on him and how he was in a really bad place when he came to visit me last year. He took all the blame, apologized for how he treated me and regretted the role he played in allowing the enemy to use him to disrupt my life. It turned out to be a very good healing conversation for me. I'm glad my guards let him through! I needed to see that someone was sincerely sorry for what they did to me. It provided some closure that I really needed.

Journal Thoughts:

- Have you ever been hurt by someone you trusted but they never apologized? How does that make you feel? Can you forgive and find closure without having an apology?

- Read Ephesians 4:31-32 and write about how that scripture makes you feel. Are there times you treat others bad because of past hurts that are inside of you? Is it easy for you to be kind to those who hurt you? What is one thing you can do that will show compassion to someone who has hurt you?

JOURNAL YOUR JOURNEY

MARRY GO ROUND

Two years after the situation with Todd, I had the opportunity to go on a mission trip to Namibia, Africa with a group from my church. We worked with an organization that sent us into the schools to talk about abstinence. AIDS is a huge problem in Africa and the government knew that safe sex was not protecting people from contracting HIV. Abstinence was the only thing that would help stop the spread; and they were willing to let us go in and spread the Gospel as long as we taught about abstinence, as well. It was an awesome opportunity. It was also a trip that would change my life forever.

It was on this trip that I felt God calling me to share my testimony about being abused for the first time. I was so afraid. I was afraid of what my team would think of me. I was afraid that my story would have no meaning for anyone else. Thank God He knew better and had a purpose for me sharing my story. I shared my story multiple times; and every time I shared it, a girl would come up to me to tell her own story of abuse. One girl shared how she had been raped multiple times and lived in a home where she was blamed for everything that happened to her. My story helped many girls realize it wasn't their fault. It restored hope and value in them, as well. I couldn't help but feel somewhat convicted, though. Here I was worrying about what they would all think of me – almost to the point of keeping everything to myself. I wasn't believing the thing that I taught them. I wasn't believing in my own worth. I realized I still had a lot to work on.

I built a lot of amazing friendships on that trip. One of those friendships was with a young woman named Jen. About a year and a half later, Jen had gotten married to a guy in the Air Force. While stationed at Aviano Base in Italy, they became friends with a guy named Ben. Jen thought we had a lot in common and suggested that he and I get to know each other better. We spent a few months in my safe place: talking on the phone and emailing. We even had dates where we would rent the same movie, talk on the phone before watching it and then call each other when the movie was done to discuss it! It was sweet. Here I was again in yet another relationship that couldn't be affected by being in one another's physical presence. This always made it easier for me to get to know the person I was dating. After all, he lived on a completely different continent! He loved the Lord so much and had dreams of being a missionary. There are so many details to Ben, but I'll do my best to make a long story short.

When Thanksgiving rolled around, Ben decided to fly to Ohio to visit me a week before the holiday. When I saw him for the first time in the airport, I thought I would feel my heart flutter. I worried a little when I didn't, but he was in the states now, so I knew I needed to make the best out of the situation. We spent the week together talking and getting to know each other even better. He knew all the good and bad about me and still wanted to pursue the relationship. Physically, the most he did was hold my hand which, to me, meant he respected me. In my mind, I thought he had to be the one.

After staying with me for a week, he flew to California to see his family. A few days later, I flew out to spend an extended Thanksgiving weekend with his family. I had my doubts, but I was 30 years old at this point. I figured I would never find anyone else to marry; and Ben checked the boxes well enough. Thanksgiving night, we went to see the new James Bond movie. We got to the theater really early because we thought there would be a line for tickets, but there wasn't. We ended up sitting in his car and having a long talk. We decided that we were not going to say "I love you" unless it was followed by a proposal. Those were words that you can't take lightly. Those were words I still wasn't sure I fully understood. The conversation went in many directions, but it ended with Ben telling me that he didn't think he was capable of love. My heart sunk deep into my chest.

I went to sleep that night trying to plan out how I was going to tell him that I couldn't keep going in a relationship that wasn't going to end in marriage. The next morning, he had plans to go Christmas shopping. We were going to celebrate Christmas early with his family since he was leaving to go back to Italy. When he got back home, he came into the bathroom where I was putting on makeup and kissed my forehead. I was shocked because he had never been that intimate with me. I wasn't really sure what to think. After everyone exchanged gifts, we decided to go have lunch on the beach and end the night with a bonfire. He asked me if I wanted to go on a walk while his family prepared the food. I had always dreamed of walking down the beach with a guy who loved me. The thing is, I was walking down the beach with a guy that I knew was about to break up with me. As we were walking, I would wince every few steps from the sharp, broken shells under our feet. Who knew feeling the sand beneath your toes could be so hazardous! We laughed as we tried to find a spot with no sharp shells. He told me that after our conversation the night before, he sat on the couch, prayed and read scripture all night. He had found some passages on love and started reading them to me. He then said the last thing I had expected him to say:

> "Mindee as I read about what love is, I realized that I love you."

What?!! We both agreed that neither of us would say that unless it was followed by a proposal. As I looked up, he got down on one knee and pulled out an engagement ring. I was in utter shock. I had been preparing my heart to end the relationship all day and he pulls this! Was he really asking me to spend the rest of my life with him? I had to say "Yes," right? I heard a whisper in my ear telling me this may be the only chance I have to get married... and I listened. With a smile that went from ear to ear, I replied: "Yes!" There wasn't a "watermelon" to be found anywhere near my response this time! It turns out he hadn't been completely honest with me. When he had gone out to do his Christmas shopping, he called my Dad to ask for permission to propose to me. With my father's approval, he then completed his holiday shopping with a stop to the jeweler's to buy me a ring. When we got back to his family and told them, they were as shocked as I was. And just like that, out of the clear blue sky, I had my own romantic proposal on the beach. As crazy as it sounds, all I could feel in my heart was confusion followed by that ever-escaping feeling that I was finally worth something. That someone actually wanted to spend the rest of their life with me.

The next morning, we got up early because Ben was taking me to Disneyland. One thing you must understand about me is that I love all things Disney (Space Mountain not included!). I had been to Disney World multiple times, but I had never been to Disneyland; so this was a pretty big deal. We had so much fun! I kept finding myself putting my hand out so I could see the ring on my finger. Towards the end of the night, we found ourselves standing under a dimming sky watching fireworks. As they were ending, snow began to fall as the speakers serenaded us with romantic music. Technically, it was really foam because we were in California and it wasn't even cold, but you get the point! The moment was picture perfect. I had managed to sneak the hundredth look at my ring when, as I looked back up at him, he leaned down and kissed me. This was our first romantic kiss… and I was on cloud nine! He had waited for and respected me; and I had never been more comfortable.

The next day, Ben and I both went our separate ways.

Ben flew back to Italy while I headed back to Ohio. I started planning for the wedding as soon as my plane touched down. Though wedding planning should've been a happy occasion, it felt weird because I was depressed and upset all the time. I didn't know why. Everyone kept reminding me how thrilled I should be, but I wasn't. I consulted a wedding planner for renting out a reception hall and mapping out when the invitations should be sent out. Instead of being relieved to have such huge benchmarks checked off the list, all I could do was cry. Right after Christmas, Ben started acting weird, too. He would go days without talking to me. Often, he wouldn't even respond to my emails. I was beyond baffled. Then, right before New Year's, Ben called and told me he just couldn't marry me. He said the proposal had been a mistake and that he felt he wasn't supposed to get married. His words have been forever burned into my memory:

"I can't marry you."

Every ounce of worth I had felt like it'd been burned up in a fire. I couldn't breathe. I couldn't think. I just felt pain. I struggled with anxiety and depression in ways I had never known before. Looking back now, I understand that I knew before Ben even proposed that we weren't supposed to be together. That's why I was so miserable trying to plan our wedding. Going back even further, that's why my heart didn't flutter when he stepped off that plane and we met face-to-face for the first time. Though I was able to piece it all together in hindsight, in that moment, all I kept processing more than anything else was rejection. He made me feel like

I was worth something and then took it away. I had grabbed ahold of what he'd given me so tightly that when I lost him, I lost myself. I struggled for a long time with what my purpose was as I turned 31 years old. For someone who just wanted to be a mom and wife, it was beginning to feel like it would never happen.

So, what's the point of telling you this part of my story that didn't have a happy ending? Well, it's clearly not over yet; but the entire point of my book is to be painfully transparent in hopes that it helps you either figure out or avoid similar downfalls. My downfall with Ben was one that I had been revisiting throughout my life. I kept placing my worth in the feeble hands of what another human being thought of me. There's not one person on this earth who can tell you your worth. Only one Being knows and bestows your value: the One Who created you. Believing God in His Word regarding how much of a treasure you are has to be sufficient enough for you so that you don't keep fishing for it in other places; but that's so much easier said than done. Believe me, I know.

This is where I would say I hit rock bottom. I gave up for about a year after Ben called off the wedding. It was at this point that I begged God to tell me why my life had to be so hard. Why I was never good enough for anyone… including Him. No matter how hard I tried being what everyone wanted me to be, no one wanted me. It's so easy to look at someone else and dream about having their life so that you're not miserable in your own. It seems things are always greener on the other side, right? The thing is, we don't see what's making their side greener: plenty of manure! I grew up in a time when Diana became the Princess of Wales. I watched her wedding on television. I dreamed of being a princess. I, like so many young girls, dreamed of being her. She was beautiful! She was adored everywhere she went. I wanted to be adored like that! Then we all found out that she had been miserable from the moment she got engaged. It came out that the Prince was having an affair throughout their entire marriage. Despite having everything I thought I wanted, she still felt unloved, uncared for and despised. She suffered from bulimia and had tried taking her own life several times. When your identity is found in everything and everyone else besides God, you can have everything you've ever dreamed of and still be miserable.

The anxiety I felt was so bad, I couldn't go anywhere without my heart feeling like it was going to explode. Anytime I was around a lot of people, my heart would start to race and I would get lightheaded. The only places I mustered enough strength to go to were work and church, occasionally. It was all so physically exhausting. Yet and still, my rest was torturous in its own right. When I did actually sleep, I would have nightmares or would wake up with my mind racing. I began drinking several glasses of wine before I went to bed to induce an uninterrupted sleep state. My friends and family became very worried about me. My brother Randy took me on a trip to Florida to try and help me get my mind off of everything. My friends tried loving me in every way they knew how, but my heart was broken. I felt broken. I felt unlike my true self. I felt…

"unmended."

I eventually agreed to start meeting with one of my Bible study leaders. Rhonda and I would go on long walks in places where we were the only two around. Those walks produced two conversations that were pretty pivotal in my healing. The first talk we had centered around the following question:

> "If you were to die today and end up at the pearly gates, what would you say when God asked you why you should be let into heaven?"

Heavy, right?!! I answered her in the only way I could at that moment. I brought up all of the things I had done that were pleasing to God like studying His Word and striving to be more like Him. She looked at me for a bit then followed up her question by asking if I had grown up Catholic. I couldn't figure out why on earth she had asked me that. I grew up in a Christian school. I had gone to church my whole life and I knew a lot of scripture. Never once had I thought of myself as Catholic. Then I realized that everything I had said was about doing good things to get into heaven. Indeed, that was a very Catholic response!

I knew what Ephesians 2:8-9 stated. I knew that it isn't works or things we do that get us into heaven. So, why on earth had I said that?!! As I worked my way through it, I realized that I believed God's truth for everyone else but myself. I thought I had to be perfect for God to give me the desires of my heart. If I studied and memorized enough scripture, if I helped enough people come to know Him; then maybe I would be worthy of God's love symbolized by my entrance into the pearly gates of heaven. But what about my abuse? Could all of my works undo the role I had been tricked into believing I played in being abused? Could my works balance this out? This logic was both faulty and the furthest thing from the truth. Ephesians 2:8-9 says:

> "For it is by grace you have been saved, through faith – and this is not from yourselves, it is the gift of God – not by works, so that no one can boast." (NIV)

All I had to do was believe in Who God is and that He sent His Son Jesus to die for me. By His grace, I am saved; and that's all it takes for me to go to heaven. The only thing I had to do is believe. The only thing you have to do… is believe.

The second conversation I had with Rhonda focused on how I just felt like God wasn't there. The moment after Ben broke up with me, I told my Mom to just turn on some worship music. Leading up to this moment with Rhonda, I tried finding God in the scriptures I read and prayers I spoke, but it felt like God just wasn't there. He promised He would never leave me or forsake me… so, where was He? Why couldn't I hear Him? She answered with a modern-day parable about a pilot flying in his airplane. When there's a storm and all he hears is the rain pounding on a window he can no longer see out of, how is he still able to fly the plane? He relies on the instruments. The instruments tell him the truth of where he is and tell him where to go. Even when I can't hear or feel God I can always rely on the instrument of scripture. It is the one thing that will tell me the truth about who I am and what I should do.

I went back to scripture and prayed armed with this insight, but I still felt purposeless. One day, I was sitting at my desk at work when I remember saying out loud:

> "God, what do You want me to do?"

I heard a voice say as clear as day:

> "Mindee, I want you to move to Chicago and live with your brother. I want you to go back to school and work for a church."

I looked around because I really thought someone was in the room talking to me. Someone had spoken to me, alright... and it was God! I had gone so long without hearing Him that when I did finally, I recognized His voice right away (even if it did startle me, initially!). In that moment, I felt two things. I felt relief because everything I knew to be true about God felt totally real. He had never left me. I knew He had been right by my side all these years guiding me along. And in that moment, just like the pilot's flight instruments, He was telling me to change course. I didn't know what was in store for me in Chicago. All I knew was that His love for me was real, and deep; and that He was going to get me through my pain.

Before God could get me through the pain, He was going to need to get me through the fear that began setting in. My thoughts immediately turned to what I would be leaving. I didn't want to move away from my family, friends and everything I'd ever known in my hometown. Technically, that wouldn't be entirely the case. My brother Randy had moved to a suburb of Chicago. That didn't matter, though. My obedience was key because if there's one thing I know for sure, it's this: When God tells you to do something and you don't obey, you're sure to miss out on the plans He has to give you peace and an expected end (see Jeremiah 29:11-12). Besides, God's promise to make a great nation out of Abram and bless him was conditional to him separating from his family like God told him (see Genesis 12:1-2). Within days, I had worked things out with my family and put in my two weeks at work. Though I had found a place to live, I hadn't quite worked out where I would go back to school or find work yet. I knew I wanted to study how to counsel others who had been through what I had been through so that I could help girls like me who had been hurt. I also knew I loved helping people see the hope God has given us in the face of the struggles we endure. That's all I needed to take with me. And just like that... I was off to Chicago!

The first thing I found was an adult accelerated program for a B.A. in Human Services at Judson University. It seemed catered to what I wanted to do because it covered counseling, social work and human resources. With that under my belt, I would have what I needed to go on for my Masters. Next, I found a job through a temp agency. It wasn't at a church like God had said, but I thought maybe I had simply misunderstood. I started going to the same church my brother's family attended and assumed that this would fit the bill to complete the instruction He had given me. Once I arrived at the church, I did what came easy for me: I started singing on the worship team. Life had to get better right? It couldn't get worse.

Journal Thoughts:

- If God asked you to share a low point in your story, could you do it? What dark passengers show up when you think about sharing your story? What do you hear them saying to you? Are they lies? Search scripture for some truths about the power of the testimony and write them down. Try to memorize them.

- Have you ever heard God's voice? It doesn't have to be audible like my experience. Have you ever felt His presence and knew He was talking to you? Whether or not you believed what He said, write it down. Did you believe or do what He asked you to do? If not, why? God never promised this life would be comfortable. Sometimes, we have to step out of our comfort zone in order to receive the blessings He has for us.

JOURNAL YOUR JOURNEY

FROM DARK PASSENGERS TO DARK CHOCOLATE

I didn't realize how much obeying what God told me to do would change the entire trajectory of my life. It was the scariest thing I have ever done. I was working and going to school full-time while serving at church on the weekends. Though I was very busy, I loved what I was doing! In one of my classes, we had a marriage and family therapist tell the class that anyone going into the counseling field really ought to see a therapist themselves. I hadn't done any counseling since I was eighteen with Dr. Fratzke. That seemed like a pretty logical next step since I knew I wanted to be able to help people. Plus, I knew I still had a lot of healing to do. Since I still struggled with defining myself by those around me. It was about time I fixed that.

One thing I want to point out is that not every therapist is always going to be a good fit. In fact, I've come across many therapists who've given advice that I question even to this day. Having said that, when identifying a therapist, I encourage you to:

1. Seek out a Christian therapist. Ask your church for people they would suggest.
2. Do your research. Make sure your therapist is reputable.
3. If you find a Christian therapist but don't feel

> like s/he is a good fit, please don't just stop and blame it on the therapist. Keep trying. Yes – it may mean having to repeat your story to new people which may seem very difficult; but the more you tell your story, the easier it is to name what you have been through.

The therapist I went to was very sweet and was able to get me talking about things in ways I had never thought of before. She suggested books to read and gave me assignments that would help outside of what we did while I was in her office. The thing that impacted me the most was what happened within my classes, though.

My program at Judson worked in cohorts. All this means is that the majority of people in my classes were the same students from my first class that was directly associated with my major. We all became very close. So, by the time we were halfway through our curriculum, most of them already knew my story. In fact, there was one course where we demonstrated how to use the types of therapy we were learning on one another. One of my friends wound up practicing cognitive therapy on me which is when I speak out loud to myself things that God says about me from scripture. This was the same method that Dr. Fratzke had utilized! I cried through the entire process. At 18 years of age, this approach to therapy had helped me stand beyond my obstacles. At 32 years of age, I was brought to my knees.

God continually worked on my identity until I was

willing to let go of who I thought I was supposed to be in favor of becoming more like who Christ had redeemed me to be in His resurrection. Until I accepted this version of Mindee Hill, I was always going to struggle. I almost picture it like dark chocolate M&M candy. When God created us in the beginning of the earth, we were never intended to have sin as part of who we were. Adam and Eve were sinless: they were perfect pieces of chocolate candy. Perfectly round with that perfectly chocolate taste that gives you a warm comfort when it melts in your mouth. That taste is so distinctive, you don't even have to see it to recognize the goodness. Someone could place it in your mouth while your blindfolded and you'd still know you were experiencing dark chocolate. That's what it's like being created in God's image. When God created us in His "image," I don't believe it was referring to something you could see. It was His distinct attributes imprinted on our spirit. After all, He created us in spirit form (see Genesis 1:26a) before creating a shell out of the dust of the ground to house us in (see Genesis 2:7). Can you imagine eating the hollow shell of a dark chocolate M&M? The unique taste doesn't come from the shell – it comes from within! It comes from that delectable cocoa bean that was so fearfully and wonderfully made first! Similarly, the body is nothing without the spirit.

When Adam and Eve sinned, shame came upon them while the humiliation of being seen naked drove them to clothe themselves. This covering they created translates to the hard-outer shell we still create for ourselves as we attempt to cover up for the shame of our own sins. Once it's worn long enough, we begin to forget our true identity as we mistake the shell for who we really are. We have to remember that *what* we are on the outside is not *who* we are on the inside. That chocolatey goodness that is the spirit of who we are is what needs to break out of the shell so others can taste and see the goodness of our Lord for themselves!:

> "O taste and see that the LORD is good: blessed is the man that trusteth in him." - Psalm 34:8

How can I say this another way? The more I worked on what it meant to be like the Christ inside of me, the more I became that amazing piece of dark chocolate that melts the hearts of others – releasing them to do the same!

That hard outer shell represents the outer image the world desires to consume as our identity. It consists primarily of our physical body and the facades we put on to dress it up. It is the most temporary thing about us because it diminishes over time. For women, there's the weight gained after children. There's "dad bod" that sets in as less active men continue to eat whatever they want in the same manner they did as super active younger men. Things drop, droop and sag over time. Yet and the same, this ever-changing outer shell becomes the definition of beauty. Now, don't get me wrong – there is something to be said for physical beauty. After all, it's what initially attracts us to people. The problem comes in when people only identify themselves by their outward physical body – spending more time making an outer shell perfect and not enough time working on our initial and inner beauty. That inner beauty reflects what God created in us as His likeness.

Besides, have you ever seen someone who's physically gorgeous but as you got to know them, they're really ugly on the inside? It makes you not want to be around them. We're all familiar with this cliché of a shallow person but that's not necessarily what I'm talking about. My story thus far hasn't been about how shallow I was. Many of us are walking around with our likeness to God marred. Recall every guy I encountered in my life after the abuse I experienced as a child. They couldn't see who I was on the inside because they were blinded by their physical attraction to my outer shell. There wasn't so much as a care in the world for who I was inside. Meanwhile, on my side of things, I thought their attraction to my outer appearance could somehow validate the inner me that had been scarred. I couldn't have been more wrong. When your inner beauty is more like Christ, it draws people to you that don't care about the outer shell. People with inner beauty are very easy to be around. You feel comfortable talking to them and can open up to them. Prideful people (who often put up walls to hide painful pasts of their own) are hard to be around. Most of your time with them is spent listening to them boast about themselves as a way to compensate for some type of lack or trauma in their life. You don't get much of an opportunity to talk and when you do, it's quickly turned back to them. Just remember, everyone reacts to trauma differently.

Redirecting your focus on who you are inside is a lifelong process. Before my incident with Todd, all I did was try to be more like Christ; but still I ended up in a bad situation with him. The problem was my motivation. I wasn't becoming more like Christ to just be more like Christ. I was becoming more like Christ to get what I wanted. Yes, I was growing closer to God which is always a good thing. But I was doing so to polish up that hard outer shell versus nurturing the Christ within me without any other motive besides getting to know Him. In a way, I was manipulating my relationship with God to make sure I became somebody's wife. In truth, God wanted me to realize that He had already arranged my marriage. We, His chosen people, were meant to be His wife first:

> "Behold, the days are coming, declares the LORD, when I will make a new covenant with the house of Israel and the house of Judah, not like the covenant that I made with their fathers on the day when I took them by the hand to bring them out of the land of Egypt, my covenant that they broke, though I was their husband, declares the LORD."
> - Jeremiah 31:31-32 (ESV)

> "Fear not, for you will not be ashamed; be not confounded, for you will not be disgraced; for you will forget the shame of your youth, and the reproach of your widowhood you will remember no more. For your Maker is your husband, the LORD of hosts is his name; and the Holy One of Israel is your Redeemer, the God of

the whole earth he is called... For a brief moment I deserted you, but with great compassion I will gather you." - Isaiah 54:4-5,7 (ESV)

Journal Thoughts:

- Write down 5-10 things that identify you. Are they part of that outer shell or the dark chocolate center?

- Write down 5-10 Christlike things that you want to be a part of your identity. What can you do to start making them a part of your identity now?

- Have you ever gone to counseling? If not then what is holding you back from going? Write about it and then pray that God provides you with whatever you need to help you take the next step.

JOURNAL YOUR JOURNEY

UNBROKEN

We went on a bit of a tangent towards the end of the last chapter, didn't we? Dark chocolate will do it every time! Where was I? Ah, yes. Chicago. Things were lining up for me. I was close to finishing my undergraduate degree and had already started setting my sights on attaining my Master's. It was around this time that I discovered *Healing the Wounded Heart* by Dr. Dan B. Allender. It had been recommended by my therapist.

First off, let me say that it was an amazing read as it furthered my journey towards healing. Secondly, after reading it, I began to wonder where this good doctor and author taught as a professor. Though he lived in Seattle at the time, one of the programs he had taught was at Colorado Christian University. And wouldn't you know it, that happened to be the college right down the street from my brother Eric who was living near Denver. Not only that, but my family had planned to visit my brother for Thanksgiving that year. It seemed like a golden opportunity, so I set an appointment to meet with the school. My Mom went with me to visit the campus and talk with the school counselor about the program. Everything about the program sounded great but as I was walking around campus, I heard that familiar voice again:

> "This is not what I have for you."

What?!?!?!? I had worked so hard for this degree! I had managed to a 3.81 GPA – something that I never thought I could be capable of my entire life. Are you kidding me right now, God? I was completely stumped but I knew that I had to listen. I had to be patient and know that God had a plan. If I continued to trust Him, He would continue to direct me where He wanted me to go. Lord knows I had to rely on Him because I had no clue what I could do with this degree without a Master's.

With my head still spinning, I decided to visit my guidance counselor. She gave me some personality tests which helped match my gifts and talents with good job options. At the same time, I was also preparing for a test everyone in the school had to take in order to graduate. It was a timed writing test which gave me an enormous amount of anxiety. With so much riding on me passing this test (did I mention that I had to pass it in order to graduate?!!), I couldn't help but think about my history as a nervous test-taker. It never ended well! Nevertheless, I took the test and received a letter telling me I had passed. I was so relieved! But results of this test would soon tell me something else that would shock me to no end. The letter had only told me I passed; what it didn't say was how well I did. Apparently, not only did I pass but I had one of the top three scores! My guidance counselor coupled this with the other tests I'd taken with her to inform me that my career path had become very clear: I should write and speak.

Write and speak? How would I do that? I hated writing. The only thing higher than the marks I'd received on that writing test was my anxiety level! It wasn't always that way, though. I had actually wanted to write a book when I was ten years old. I had a rough draft and everything! It was about a girl with missing jewelry. That's right – it was a jewelry heist! Not really. As it turned out, her dog had taken it. I promise you, as a five-page children's illustration book, this page turner was ahead of its time! I even sent it to a publisher I found in the back of a book from our family library. I never heard from them, but that didn't deter me. I wound up writing a play later on in high school. It was nothing "to write home about", but the blueprint of a writer was there. The design of my Maker was evident:

> "Ponder the path of your feet; then all your ways will be sure." - Proverbs 4:26 (ESV)

I had been so willing to write back then so what was stopping me now? Like many of us, years of disappointment had undermined something that God had placed inside of me.

The affirmation I needed to confirm what was developing before my very eyes came from my mentor Jill. You see, it was at this time that she approached me to write a letter to the young women she began encountering who had their own stories of sexual abuse. After I wrote it, the letter kept coming back to me with the following prompt:

> "Write a book about your journey for these girls

(and guys)."

Really God? How do I do that when I don't think I have any talent for writing? The truth of the matter is that I didn't have any talent. God had lent me a portion of His creative genius and was looking for a return on His investment (see the Parable of the Talents in Matthew 25:14-30). I decided to yield my will to His, but I did have a condition: I needed a job to support me while I wrote. I was clocking hours working at a company that I did not enjoy. God's words crystallized before me as I recalled how He had said I should work for a church once I got to Chicago. With that in mind, I applied for jobs at churches all over the country! It didn't matter if I was overqualified! I even sent applications to places that weren't even hiring just so they'd have my resume on file if a job opened up.

As I began writing, it became evident that I was still in the process of healing. To find some closure, I took some time and went back to the church where the abuse happened. I spoke with the pastor about the journey I was on. He was more than willing to help me and let me in the church on a Saturday morning which led to me to praying over those areas in the basement where the abuse happened. On the way to the church, *Healing Rain* by Michael W. Smith came on the radio. As I sat there in the car, I had a moment with Jesus. We wept. The lyrics are:

> "Healing rain is coming down
> It's coming nearer to this old town.

Rich and poor, weak and strong
It's bringing mercy, it won't be long.
Healing rain is coming down
It's coming closer to the lost and found.
Tears of joy and tears of shame
Are washed forever in Jesus' name.
Healing rain, it comes with fire
So let it fall and take us higher.
Healing rain, I'm not afraid
To be washed in Heaven's rain.
Lift your heads, let us return
To the mercy seat where time began.
And in your eyes I see the pain.
Come soak this dry heart with healing rain.
And only you, the Son of Man
Can take a leper and let him stand.
So lift your hands, they can be held
By someone greater, the Great I Am.
Healing rain, it comes with fire
So let it fall and take us higher.
Healing rain, I'm not afraid
To be washed in Heaven's rain.
To be washed in Heaven's rain.
Healing rain is falling down,
Healing rain is falling down,
I'm not afraid.
I'm not afraid."

I wasn't afraid. How could I be with this song coming

on at that exact moment? I knew God was with me. When I got to the church, I stood at the top of the steps in the same place I was told to stand as a six-year-old lookout while Micah was downstairs with my friend. Before I knew it, I found myself praying, worshipping and singing *Healing Rain* over and over as I walked through every spot in that basement where the abuse had occurred. It was such an amazing way to confront and receive closure for my past! The entire day was an important one in my story. I knew I was no longer going to look back and let my past determine who I was from this moment on. Closure is such a crucial part of the story for anyone moving from victim to victor. It's not that things became perfect after that. Satan definitely wasn't done trying to get to me. As I look back on it, the enemy definitely had developed a strategy of attack that kept catching me off guard in the place I was supposed to feel safest: the church.

I mentioned before that I was on the worship team at my church. The church I attended in the Chicago suburbs was pretty big. It didn't matter, though – the devil still found a way to focus in on me. One weekend when I was singing as a background vocalist, I caught the attention of a guy named Gerard. I tend to smile when I'm worshipping so when Gerard saw this, he thought I was smiling directly at him. I don't know if you've ever been on a brightly lit stage but it's almost impossible to see the faces in the audience. It's definitely not possible to distinguish one out of a thousand faces in a crowd. I say that to set the stage for his reaction. Though there was no way I could have intentionally singled him out with a smile, he took it as a sign that I liked him. Unfortunately, Gerard suffered from bipolarism and psychosis which affected how he reacted to things and people he encountered. After service, he had one of his friends ask me if I wanted to go out with him. The old me would have gone out with him because I would have felt bad denying him. With the new me growing stronger, I let Gerard's friend know that while I appreciated the offer, I was not interested.

This didn't stop Gerard. He found my email and sent me messages constantly. Hoping he would get the hint, I completely ignored them. That's when things escalated. He started sending me emails about conversations he had with Satan about me. Yes. You read right. I guess the devil decided to move from behind the scenes to being front and center to deal with this new and improved version of Mindee! He went into detail about how I needed to come live with him because that was the only way I'd be protected from what Satan was about to do to the world. As you can imagine, this started making me nervous. I decided to respond with a firm request that he stop emailing me, but to no avail. I showed the emails to my close friend's boyfriend. He was the head of security for the church and a former police detective. When I asked him what he thought I should do, he consulted a current police detective who encouraged me to talk with the State Attorney's office. Long story short, I ended up filing a restraining order against Gerard.

Cyber Stalking was becoming a rising issue around that time, so they also suggested I file charges against him as a way to help set a precedence for other cases. I didn't want him to go to jail because of his condition, I just wanted him to get help and leave me alone! Things got so stressful though, I often found myself looking over my shoulder. So, to protect the precious peace of mind that I finally had after so many years, I wound up pressing charges. Gerard pleaded guilty which meant I didn't have to testify. He was sentenced to two years of Target Abuser Call supervision whereby he couldn't have any with contact me via phone, email or in-person. I had started writing this book around this time, so it became a big distraction for me. However, it fits into my story well to reinforce how the gains you make will still be tested. There's no need to fear the test, though – when you are rooted in the Lord, old footholds are transformed into fortifications!

Dating still proved to be a tricky minefield for me to maneuver, as well. While I had more confidence in myself, the creeps were still out there. There was the one guy who, like so many who had come before him, knew everything to say to make my heart melt. He was a sweetie! He was even honest enough with me to tell me he'd gone through a divorce. Come to find out, he wasn't divorced and lied to me about pretty much everything else. It was beyond exhausting for me to keep wasting time getting to know the same type of guy. You know, the one who keeps decorating his outer shell so he can pawn it off on you as his dark chocolate center? I don't know how the M&Ms snuck back in there but you get it! I was honestly ready to swear off dating altogether.

And then I met Jeff. I was very skeptical and cynical at first. I didn't even want to go out with him, but there was something undeniable that drew me to him. Our first date was just supposed to be over a cup of coffee. As the conversation grew, we found ourselves pouring a second cup which then led to bowling followed by dinner. To say that Jeff was different than any other guy I had dated would be a disservice to Jeff. He was upfront and honest. He told me he was looking for a spouse and that if I wasn't looking for the same level of commitment, he wasn't interested. He was on a mission! He had children and was doing the best he could as a single father to raise them in the Christian faith. This meant that the most important things to him were his relationship with God and his two kids. I sat there amazed as he laid it all out there because that was all I desired. Not just marriage but someone that was straight and to the point: no guile. It didn't come off as a sales pitch that he would bait and switch once I fell hook, line and sinker. He was already prepared to cut the line if I couldn't handle what he was out to catch! I had experienced enough to discern a good from a bad thing. I know Proverbs 18:22 says that he who finds a wife finds a good thing – but this?!! Jeff was a good thing! I had found my worth in Christ in Chicago. I could honestly write another book on our courtship – it definitely warrants one, but for the sake of staying on task for this book, I'll fast track the rest of our story. We were engaged within three months and married six months after that. God even used Jeff's job to bring us back to Ohio to close out my stint in Chicago. Clearly, His hand was in the entire process.

At 36 years of age, I became a wife and full-time stepmom to a 12 and 13-year-old. That wasn't easy (understatement of the year!) but I love Madison and Mason as if they are my own. Two years later, I would come to know the fullness of that as-if-they-were-my-own type of love when Jeff and I welcomed Levi into our family. And just like that, I finally had all of my desires. Life up to that point had been full of challenges and distractions, but like Job, I had come out better for it and more fulfilled on the other end. Yet, I still had some unanswered questions and needs. As a supportive wife and mother of three, I needed to get a job! I sent out resumes to Christian schools that I figured they could use someone with my degree. When no one responded, I reminded God what He told me as I questioned His next move. What was all that about working for a church? Why couldn't I pursue a Master's degree? Why did I have to settle for a degree that I can't do anything with?

Then the day came when things started to come together. I got a call from a local church that needed someone to work in their Human Resources department. They had been given my name by one of the schools I sent my resume to during my first job search. I ended up getting the job and loved it more than I ever thought I could. As I took a step back to look over the past few years, the big picture had become clear. I had come full circle. God showed me how He took me to Chicago to receive healing that I wouldn't have received in Ohio. He took me to a school that had a program which showed me how to teach that healing process to others in such a way that supported the psychological component with my Christian faith. This then prepared me for a job in the church of my home state that positions me to serve my community with all that God deposited within me – both the good and the bad! God had a plan for me from the very beginning; I was just too close to see it. There had never been a moment where He wanted me to lose my hope. I just had to depend on and trust in Him to endure!

So, what's my life like now? There are peaks and valleys, highs and lows. Through them all, I've learned to praise the Lord. We live in a fallen world full of disappointments and tragedy. I've still felt alone at times even with my husband and children. Though that is an obvious valley moment, we've made some amazing memories together that put us right back on top! I've lost family to dementia and friends to cancer. Specifically, I lost a close friend to cancer by the name of Kathy. Kathy and I bonded during my mission trip to Namibia. So much so, that even after we got back to the states, we led many Bible studies and travelled at length together. She walked with me through a lot of heartache. She would pray and cry with me then turn around and encourage me. She let me know over and over again that no matter where I have been, what I have done or what has happened to me, I am loved and whole because of Christ. Right before meeting Jeff, I took a few weeks to visit Kathy at a condo she had purchased in Maui. There were many significant moments that we shared. My time with Kathy here solidified some of the greatest stages of healing in my life. In fact, I don't believe I would have been ready to meet and commit to Jeff had it not been for this period in my life. To give you the full context of a lasting memory I will always cherish from my time with Kathy, I need to take you back to Chicago for a moment.

When I was living in Chicago, I had a picture of where I was in my mind and where I wanted to be. All the adversity I had been through had been like stones of varying sizes. Yet, as I encountered each stone, what eventually stood before me was a wall of strength built from the rocks I'd gathered through my journey. Flowing freely over this stone wall like life-giving water was a river of God's healing. He was covering all my pain and sadness with His grace and love.

It's funny how a memory from Chicago set up another memory in Maui. Truly, the Lord works in mysterious ways! Kathy wanted to take as many pictures as she could while we were reunited. I've never felt comfortable in front of cameras, but I wanted to honor her wish, so off we went to find the most picturesque spots this Hawaiian island had to offer. While we were figuring out where to go to first, the picture of the waterfall came flooding back to my mind. When I asked her if there was a waterfall anywhere on the island, she knew just the place. When we got there, I stood in front of that waterfall with my arms raised up and a huge smile on my face. God had given me a prophetic vision that had just been fulfilled. Lost in that moment, all my insecurities about taking pictures were washed away.

I lost Kathy to cancer in 2019. She was a rock for everyone who was around her. She wanted everything she did to point to Christ. Even in her cancer, she wanted to suffer well so that others could see Christ in her. I pray that I can take on her attributes. In fact, I know that I can because the same Christ that was in her resides in me. He resides in you, too. This is why I pray that my story can help others the way that she helped me. She was a perfect example of what I want to be for you. If you have someone in your life that wants to help and love on you, let them! Don't block out the people who can help you heal. You can't do it on your own. If you don't have anyone, pray God brings them into your life. He will, but you must keep your eyes open. Sometimes they show up in ways you might not expect.

Kathy's words proved to be true through the picture she had taken. It perfectly captured and presented to the world that I was not a broken girl. I was free! Free from allowing the enemy to have a foothold in my life. Free from the pain of sexual abuse. I had built strength from fighting those dark passengers that had intended to take me out. I saw myself in front of that waterfall with my arms raised high because I had freedom, strength and courage. That strength was not my own, though:

> "But he said to me, 'My grace is sufficient for you, for my power is made perfect in weakness.' Therefore, I will boast all the more gladly of my weaknesses, so that the power of Christ may rest upon me. For the sake of Christ, then, I am content with weaknesses, insults, hardships, persecutions, and calamities. For when I am weak, then I am strong."
> - 2 Corinthians 12:9-10 (ESV)

Lastly, I was courageous because I wasn't willing to let the enemy win. I fought with all I had in me and I won!:

> "Little children, you are from God and have overcome them, for he who is in you is greater than he who is in the world." - 1 John 4:4 (ESV)

That doesn't mean that those dark passengers don't rear their ugly heads every now and then. I just know how to handle them now. I memorize and speak many of the scriptures I've quoted in this book. I worship... Oh, how I love to worship! When I feel anxiety and fear come on, I sing praises to God! I worship Him through song, and it draws me closer to Him because He inhabits the praises of His people (see Psalm 22:3). Then there's the name of Jesus. When I'm really stressed about finances or problems I can't control at home and work, I just start calling out the name of Jesus. The enemy can't stand to hear or be near the name of Jesus, so I say it out loud as part of my battle cry.

Journal Thoughts:

- Is there an area where you feel the enemy attacks you over and over? Write about it. What scripture can you find that will help you the next time he attacks? Memorize it.

- Do you have hope? If so, write about it and get excited over it. If not, what is holding you back from having hope?

- If God were the author of your story, what do you think your story would be?

- Now read what you just wrote and determine if what you wrote shows God's grace or if you wrote as if it is God's wrath. What is keeping you from seeing you deserve God's grace?

- Finally, let God show you a vision of you being triumphant over your circumstances. Take some time to write down what you see.

JOURNAL YOUR JOURNEY

EPILOGUE

"For I know the plans I have for you, declares the Lord, plans to prosper you and not to harm you, plans to give you hope and a future."
– Jeremiah 29:11 NIV

Many times, the purpose of this scripture is taken out of context. I'm only going to spend a little time on this because I believe it is important; but I encourage you to research it more FOR yourself.

The book of Jeremiah was written during a time when the Israelites were being held captive by the Babylonians. Their captivity wasn't just for a few days; it was for seventy years. I don't know if you've ever known someone who did an extended bid in prison, but letters become like lifelines to inmates who might not see the light of day for a while. If you can imagine being taken from your homeland for so long that even your children were born into captivity and lived long enough to have children of their own born into captivity, then you can imagine that such a person or people may need some encouragement from time to time. Jeremiah wrote this letter with that purpose in mind: to provide hope to his people. If you read the whole chapter, you'll see Jeremiah instructing them to build homes, start families and pray for peace. He also warned them not to listen to false prophets who spoke things into their lives who were not speaking revelation from God. In other words, he was telling them to watch out for lies! We all have people who come into our lives and feed us lies that can destroy who we are if we chose to believe them. That's what I had done for most of my life.

Jeremiah even prophesied how long they would be in captivity according to what the Lord spoke to him but that they were to not lose hope because he had promised to bring them out of captivity at the end of the seventy years. This is where verse eleven of chapter twenty-nine comes in when God, through the prophet Jeremiah, tells them that He knows the plans He has for their lives. The next few words vary from translation to translation, so let's go to the original Hebrew text. The word "prosper" in the NIV text is actually the word "shalom" which means "peace." It can also be translated as:

- completeness
- wholeness
- harmony
- fulfillment

God is saying that His plans are for complete wholeness, harmony and fulfillment. If you knew that the Creator of the universe cared enough about you to promise that to you, wouldn't that bring you some peace?!! Jeremiah was reminding them to believe in God's word for them. He knew that they could do what they were called to do no matter how hard it got or what they had previously done that landed them in captivity. God could redeem their time all while being there with them every step of the way. If we have a personal relationship with God, He is that type of presence and provider in our lives. He has a plan for our future; and everything we go through in this life is part of that plan.

God took what the enemy meant for evil in my life and used it for His good. A part of His good is *your* well-being! God has a plan for your life. You can either let the enemy have control and ruin you or turn everything over (submit) to God Who already has the victory. Victory implies warfare, though. Rough terrain is ahead. As you decide to stand up to the enemy, it will definitely begin to feel like the road less travelled. But if you start at whatever point you are in your life, Satan will have no foothold. He will have no right to keep you down or stand in the way of your healing.

This is my story. In seeing God's hand in it, I pray that you will begin to know that God has His hand in your story, too. He wants you to have hope! He wants you to have victory! He wants you to find freedom in forgiveness and a fulfilling life in His name.

It may start with accepting Jesus in your heart. Maybe you've never done that and need to experience His love for yourself. If you've never had a chance to confess with your mouth what you have come to believe in our heart concerning Jesus being the Lord of your life, I encourage you to pray this right now:

> 'Dear Lord Jesus, I know that I am a sinner and I ask for Your forgiveness. I believe You died for my sins and rose from the dead. I turn from my sins and invite You to come into my heart and life. I want to trust and follow You as my Lord and Savior. Amen."

That's it! You are a child of God Who is with you on this journey to healing.

It may start with accepting what has happened to you. Remember - you need to name it! I was sexually abused. If you can't name it, you can't claim it! What you're claiming possession of is not the abuse itself. Once you name it, you are separating your God-given identity from it. What you *are* claiming is you healing from it. This may start with taking a step of faith by telling a trusted person what happened to you. Whatever you do, I just ask that you take one step that you haven't taken before. Most importantly, don't take it on your own. Have someone who is more mature in their faith who can pray with and for you. Someone you can trust to help you with enough faith to be strong when you are not.

Can you imagine how different my story would have been if I told someone what happened to me sooner? Can you see the hurt I could've avoided if I would have kept going in my healing process instead of starting and stopping multiple times over 25 years? If I would have told Jill or Sharlene what happened to me, I know things would have been different. That can't be different for me, but it can be for you. Learn from my failure patterns. Break the cycle of shutting people out after talking to them. I always ended up trying to do it on my own. Don't let Satan win that battle through isolation! He wants you alone so he can destroy any hope growing within you! If you have no one safe in your life, then find a local church and seek help there. Don't start and stop with the reading of this book! Please know, I am here to pray for you. If I can make it through this, then I know you can make it through this without having to be broken by this for the rest of your life. I felt broken for most of my life, but I can now say that I am not a broken girl! Put the brakes on letting the enemy break you! The longer you wait, the harder it is to take the next step. So… what step are you going to take right now?

Journal Thoughts:

- Do you feel broken? Write about that brokenness.

- Is the enemy winning a battle in your life? If so, what is that battle?

- What step can you take today that will help end the cycle of brokenness?

- Have you named what happened to you yet? When you are ready, name these things out loud:

- "I was or am being sexually abused."
- "I am not responsible for the crime committed against my body. It is not my fault!"
- "I am worthy of working through the abuse that damaged me."
- "I cannot keep the abuse done to me secret and I cannot allow the shame to overtake me."

— Review all the questions you've journaled since you began reading this book. Have any of your answers changed? Have you found healing? Don't let your story end here. Pray about sharing it to give others hope, but never share it unless you feel safe. Let your story have purpose!

JOURNAL YOUR JOURNEY

ADVICE FOR YOUTH LEADERS

Males Can Be Victims, Too

I was a youth leader for 13 years. Within that time span, I worked with many teen girls who had dealt with some form of sexual, physical and emotional abuse. Those external abuses opened the door to internal issues such as eating disorders, low self-esteem and various phobias. While our perspective as young girls and women has the largest percentage of reported cases, please don't overlook the fact that young boys and men can be victims of abuse, as well. Keeping this in mind, the signs and lessons learned from my story can be universally applied whether or not the youth you mentor is male or female. Abuse doesn't happen to girls or boys – it happens to *individuals*.

Know When to Be Quiet

That said, there are a few things you should always think of when working with an individual who is coming to you for either advice (when you provide a response to what they're telling you) or even just a shoulder to cry on (when you take in what they're telling you in confidence and restraint). If you're unable to tell whether or not you should respond verbally when they're confiding in you, it's best to gauge the manner in which they're telling you their story. Some may be really forthcoming while others may withdraw after opening up. If it begins to feel like your pulling teeth getting them to talk, it's okay to be comfortable in the silence. The trauma they've experienced resulted from someone forcing them to do something they didn't want to do. The last thing they need is for you to put them back in that position. Either way, never assume what you have the authority to do in responding to them. It's always best to ask what it is they want from you: an open ear to hear or an open mouth to advise. James 1:19 says it this way:

> "My dear brothers and sisters, take note of this: Everyone should be quick to listen, slow to speak and slow to become angry," (NIV)

Take note of being quick to listen and slow to speak. Let them talk at their own pace.

Avoid Blunt Confrontation

If you're seeing some of the symptoms of sexual abuse that I mentioned earlier in this book (see chapter 6) and you want to inquire further to see if abuse has occurred, tread carefully. Don't come straight out and ask if they've been sexually abused. That may work in some instances, but it may also cause the person to retreat into their shell. If the reaction is adverse enough, it may even cause them to become extremely defensive. This is especially true if they've been blaming themselves or haven't fully accepted that they have been abused.

Don't Be Too Quick to Make a Promise

It is *extremely* important that you never promise someone that you'll keep things between the two of you... no matter what it is they want to tell you. I had a situation where a girl came to me and told me she wanted to tell me something, but she wanted me to promise not to tell. My default reaction was to assume something serious had happened to her. I'm willing to make a promise if I must, but not without hearing the situation first. After all, one of the biggest things violated in abuse cases is the victim's truth. In this scenario, it wasn't what I thought it was going to be. She proceeded to tell me about how she snuck out of the house in the middle of the night to meet up with a guy. How could I keep that a secret when it could lead to repeated behavior which increases the chances of her being assaulted? Due to the potential harm she could experience, I had to tell her parents. I did lose her trust in the process but my relationship to her was as a youth leader, not her friend. You can always give them the disclaimer that you have a responsibility to your position that may require you to say something based on the situation; just don't get in the habit of promising secrecy before you've been given a chance to hear what the individual has been hiding.

Know Your State

Each state has different people who are required to

report cases of abuse. As a youth leader or friend, you are typically not mandated by law to report what you are told. If someone you know is being hurt or harmed, seek advice from a professional (lawyer, government official, police, etc.) about if and how you would go about reporting abuse to the authorities.

Comfort Comes First

When talking with individuals, make sure you're developing a safe and comfortable environment. Let them know you care about and want to be there for them. Make it clear that there's nothing they can say that would change the way you see them. Many times, victims are threatened or bribed to keep silent. The best way to break that method of control is to build a safe place for them over time. Don't rush the process. Also, don't be disappointed if they don't come out and tell you everything right away. Just pray that God would soften their hearts as you grow in patience and self-control (two of the nine fruit of the Spirit in Galatians 5:22-23).

Lastly, instruction doesn't take away pain so avoid the urge to instruct them in the early stages of them entrusting you (see 2 Corinthians 1:1-7). Simply stated, comfort takes away pain more than instruction ever could.

Don't Put Words in Their Mouths

If an individual has already admitted or eluded to the fact that they've been sexually abused, then there are a few things to keep in mind. Do not try to direct or instruct them on what they should say or how they say it. This creates a different narrative that ends up being in your words and not their own. Instead, ask them open ended questions, such as:

> "Can you tell me how it started?"
>
> "What happened next?"
>
> "How did/does that make you feel?"

By the way, these questions are actually good initiators for any counseling session!

Be Emotionally Available

Be alert to their feelings and how they are suffering. At any given moment, they may need someone who is willing to be hurt with or even cry for them. There may be times when they become angry. Don't try to diffuse it. Let them feel. They need to get those feelings and emotions out that they might have been bottling up and carrying around for years. Scream with them if need be – as long as it's genuine. Let them know that what happened to them upsets you as well.

They just want someone to love them despite the shame they're feeling. Now is not the time to preach! Preaching to them will not cast out their fear. Only love can do that:

> "There is no fear in love, but perfect love casts

out fear. For fear has to do with punishment, and whoever fears has not been perfected in love." - 1 John 4:18 (ESV)

Show them care before telling them what they need to do. The day I first told Dr. Fratzke what happened to me, she just loved on me. If she would have automatically started telling me what to do before developing a bond with me, I would have shut down.

Be Aware of Your Body Language

Non-verbal communication can be a deal breaker! This may sound weird but your office is an extension of your body language! Make sure your office is as open as you want to be for the person you're counseling. When they come into your space, make sure there's nothing between the two of you. When at all possible, don't sit behind a desk while they sit in front of it. That comes off as you being distant. Reduce distractions like loud music or other people in the room. Put your laptop, cell phone, iPad, desktop on pause! Silence whatever device with the potential to send you a notification that will make you want to pick it up or glance over at it. Why? It is critical to make and maintain eye contact. Breaking eye contact too often or for extended periods of time gives the impression that you have better things you'd rather be doing. Stay in the moment! Nod your head. Lean forward to show you're interested and that they have your undivided attention. Remember the fruit of the Spirit I mentioned earlier: patience? When silent moments arise because they don't know what to say, the virtue of patience sometimes begins to look like what the King James Version calls this particular fruit: longsuffering! Don't let your body language communicate that you are suffering in their silence! Learn to wait without leading them.

Affirmative Action

Be sure to affirm them throughout the conversation. Victims of sexual abuse need frequent and sincere affirmation. Saying things like "I would have felt the same way" or "I'm glad you said that" affirm who they are on the inside. Such assurances validate their reactions to trauma. Don't hold back on expressing love and appreciation for them. Let them know that you understand how hard it must be to share what they've been through. Let them hear from your mouth how very strong and courageous they are to talk about it now. It may seem redundant to you to continually reaffirm them but the brokenness they're overcoming can only be rebuilt one brick at a time. Each word of affirmation, no matter how repetitive it may feel, builds them up. After all, a person's soul is restored word by word in the same way that a wall is built brick by brick: repetition.

Next Steps

There are many ways to direct them once they've had a breakthrough. Whether the breakthrough happens after the first or twenty-first conversation is irrelevant. Just remember that their conversations with you are not the end of their process. While professional intervention is essential, there are still things you can do to help. Never become so prideful that you think you can do this by yourself. Know your limitations. Their next step may require a licensed professional, but if they trust you, they should be willing to allow you to help point them in the right direction. The next two sections of this book have resources to supplement your counseling sessions in the form of books and national hotline numbers.

If they insist on only seeking you for advice, begin setting them up to discover resolutions on their own. Try and get the person you're working with to answer the question: "What's next?" Try a combination of the following seven steps which I've adapted from the *Handbook on Counseling Youth* by Josh McDowell and Bob Hostetler to get them to this point:

1. Guide them to acknowledge out loud that they have been abused and identify the effects it is having in their life.

2. If the abuse is currently happening, encourage and accompany them (if necessary) to inform their parents. If you are serving as a youth leader in a church program, contact their youth pastor or whoever is in charge of the program. Even if the program is not faith-based, find out who's in charge of contacting the parents, guardians or appropriate authorities based on what's called for in that situation.

3. Help them give the responsibility back to the

abuser as opposed to taking full responsibility for being violated. This can be done by gently and consistently assuring them that "This is not your fault."

4. Turn them to God Who is the true Source of healing and wholeness. God didn't cause the trauma, but He is the solution to it.

5. Make sure they've walked through every stage of grief. Don't let them do it alone. Help them confront, express, and resolve feelings.

6. Commit to praying for and with them.

7. Encourage them that healing takes time.

For those who are currently experiencing abuse during their time with you, make sure they understand that the abuse cannot be allowed to continue under any circumstance. Confiding in you can rapidly start the healing process (as it did with me), but without continued help, it can stop just as rapidly. You may physically see the weight lifted off of their shoulders, but such burdens can just as easily be placed back on once they leave; especially if the abuse has or is still occurring in their home. The next step may be as drastic as moving out of a house or calling the police. Whatever the case may be, you need to be willing to be there for them in those next steps. If that's a responsibility that you aren't ready to take on (take a moment to honestly check your bandwidth), then be sure to explain that to them as you help them find the next level of help necessary for their process to continue. Do not leave them to their own devices!

This is where referring them to a professional therapist may come in. You may not know anyone to refer them to but seek out pastoral advice for a Christian therapist, if available. Acknowledge that you cannot provide all the help they need and that God has already gifted someone else to provide for them and their family.

BOOK SUGGESTIONS

Basic Counseling

Handbook on Counseling Youth
    by: Josh McDowell and Bob Hostetler

Instruments in the Redeemer's Hands
    by: Paul David Tripp

How People Grow
    by: Dr. Henry Cloud and Dr. John Townsend

Quick Scripture Reference for Counseling
    by: John Kruis

Quick Scripture Reference for Counseling Youth
    by: Patricia and Keith Miller

Shattered Dreams
    by: Larry Crabb

Specific to Sexual Abuse

Healing the Wounded Heart
    by: Dr. Dan Allender

Healing the Wounded Heart Workbook
   by: Dr. Dan Allender

HOTLINE NUMBERS

National Sexual Assault Hotline
1-800-656-HOPE (4673)

National Child Abuse Hotline
1-800-4-A-CHILD (422-4453)

Youth Crisis Hotline
1-800-HIT-HOME (448-4663)

Suicide Hotline
1-800-273-TALK (8255)

Eating Disorders
1-888-236-1188

Self-Injury
SAFE (Self-Abuse Finally Ends)
1-800-DONT-CUT (366-8288)

Holy Spirit Teenline
1-800-722-5385

In general, hotlines have three things in common:

They are available 24/7
They are 100% CONFIDENTIAL
They are FREE

ABOUT THE AUTHOR

Mindee Berg is a wife, mom, writer and speaker. Decades of experience in youth, music and women's ministry has afforded her the ability to offer careful encouragement, direction, hope and growth from both a Biblical and personal perspective as she helps others navigate a complex world.

Born in Dayton, Ohio, Mindee now resides in Columbus, OH with her husband Jeff along with their young son Levi and stepchildren Madison and Mason. In 1998, she received her Associate's degree in Communication from Sinclair Community College in Dayton Ohio. In 2009, she earned a Bachelor of Arts degree in Human Services from Judson University in Elgin, Illinois; as well as a Certificate in Human Behavior.

Mindee longs to see her brothers and sisters in Christ grow closer to the Lord and walk alongside them in their journey towards healing. *Not a Broken Girl* is her first venture into book publishing which she hopes will create a platform to help her fulfill that desire!

If you're in need of prayer, a speaker for youth leader training or a special youth/adult event, please contact me at: **notabrokengirl@gmail.com**.

Made in the USA
Middletown, DE
26 April 2021

38370576R00109